"In some 32 short essays on .... of modern life, Rivenbark (*Bless Your Heart, Tramp; We're Just Like You, Only Prettier*) wanders through Tweenland at the mall thinking a better name would be 'Little Skanks'...This is a hilarious read, perhaps best enjoyed while eating Krispy Kreme doughnuts with a few girl-friends." —*Publishers Weekly*

"She kills in the 'Kids' and 'Southern-Style Silliness' sections, put-ting the fear of Mickey into anyone planning a trip to Disney World (character breakfasts must be scheduled 90 days in advance) and extolling the entertainment value of obituaries ('If there's a nickname in quotes, say Red Eye, Tip Top, or simply, Zeke, then my entire day is made')." —*Entertainment Weekly*

"Celia Rivenbark has a mouth on her, but it's a very funny mouth as you will learn if you read her new book...she certainly strikes at the hilarious heart of what one often feels without being able to express in polite society. In any case, if you need down-to-earth information about celebrity babies, selling a bowl of grits on eBay that looks like Willie Nelson, or Barbie's creepy new Australian boyfriend, then Celia Rivenbark is for you." —*Daily Herald*

"Rivenbark's collection of essays will have you snorting with laughter (unless you're a deb, of course, who would never dream of snorting). It's obvious where the author stands on fashions for little girls, but she also pokes fun at the necessity of taking chil-dren—or not—to Disney World, trying to get phone assistance from people in India, hating the knitting craze, and the Southern obsession with ailments. She encourages moms to not only slow down but slack off. And she's not afraid to poke fun at rednecks." —*Daily Advertiser*

Also by Celia Rivenbark

We're Just Like You, Only Prettier

Bless Your Heart, Tramp

STOP DRESSING YOUR

Six-Year-Old

LIKE A  Skank

A Slightly Tarnished Southern Belle's
Words of Wisdom

Celia Rivenbark

St. Martin's Griffin ❧ New York

For my parents,
Howard and Caroline Rivenbark,
with love and gratitude
for never letting me look skanky

www.stmartins.com

Library of Congress Cataloging-in-Publication Data

Rivenbark, Celia.
    Stop dressing your six-year-old like a skank : a slightly tarnished southern belle's words of wisdom / Celia Rivenbark.
        p. cm.
    ISBN-13: 978-0-312-33994-4
    ISBN-10: 0-312-33994-1
    1. American wit and humor. 2. Southern states—Humor. I. Title

PN6165.R59 2006
814'.6—dc22

                                                            2006043881

First St. Martin's Griffin Edition: September 2007

10 9 8 7 6 5 4 3 2 1

Contents

Contents

Part II: Celebrities

Part III: Vanity Flares

Contents

Part IV: Huzzzbands

Part V: Southern-Style Silliness

Contents

PART I

Kids

1

There's Always Tomorrow(land)

"If You Really Loved Me, You'd Buy Me Pal Mickey"

Studies say that children don't remember all that much, and certainly nothing good, until they are at least six years old. So there was no way we were going to waste hundreds, perhaps millions, of dollars on a family trip to Disney World until Sophie could remember *in minute detail* what wonderful, generous parents we were.

That said, the trip was finally scheduled, and we began to anticipate five days and four nights of fabulous forced family fun, fun, fun! When I told another mom of our plans at a birthday party, she beamed. "Did you get the early seating at Cinderella's Gala Feast?"

"Say who?"

"The Gala Feast! What about your character breakfast? Did you book Pooh at the Crystal Palace or Pluto and Goofy at

Liberty Square or Donald and Mickey at Restaurantosaurus?"

"Huh?"

"Oh, for heaven's sake," she huffed. Turning away from me, she summoned a few of the other moms over. "She's going to Disney and she hasn't booked her character breakfasts yet."

Some of them laughed so hard, they turned inside out.

My friend Lisa whipped out her dog-eared copy of the 475-page Katie Couric–endorsed *Walt Disney World with Kids,* a book that I have since discovered is more valuable than a dime-store poncho for the wacky waterfall rides. (Sure, you could buy the officially sanctioned Disney poncho, for approximately twenty-six dollars, but why not pack the ninety-nine-cent version from Eckerd?)

"You must book these things ninety to a hundred and twenty days in advance," she said. "Do you think that tickets to the Hoop-Dee-Doo Musical Revue just fall out of the sky?"

Hoop-Dee-Do-What?

As it turns out, you must—and I am not making this up—call the Disney dining hotline at exactly 7:00 a.m. exactly ninety days ahead of time. At that moment, mommies across this great land are groggily poised over their phones in hopes of getting these in-demand seats.

"Why can't I just call at nine?" I moaned. "I'm not really a morning person."

"Well, you can," said Lisa, "but you'll end up eating

chicken out of a bucket with Sneezy. *Is that what you want? Is it?"*

I was so ashamed. Who knew?

Thank goodness I'd had this whole conversation in time to right the wrong. I hovered over my phone exactly sixty days before our trip, just as I had been told during an exploratory call to the Disney dining folks.

"Sorry, that event is ninety days out. We have nothing left," said the chirpy Disney rep.

"No, no! You told me sixty days, not ninety!"

"I'm sorry, but these things change according to season and demand. I'm afraid you'll have to eat chicken out of a bucket with Sneezy."

Good thing we've got the ponchos, I thought to myself.

The Disney wars had been raging in my little family for two years, ever since that fateful school holiday when we were the only family that didn't leave town.

When I first learned that my daughter would have a week off of kindergarten because of "spring break," I laughed so hard, I almost choked on my McRib. (Motto: "Back but still alarmingly mediocre!")

"Spring break!" I snorted. "For kindergarten?" Does a five-year-old honestly need a whole week off after a tough four months of learning to share?

Was she going to demand a trip to Daytona Beach with some gal pals, a rented convertible, and a beer bong?

What up? I asked some of the savvier moms.

"This is when you go to Disney World," they chanted in unison. Their arms shot straight out from their bodies, and they toy-soldier-marched away from me, the Clueless Mommy.

Well, Disney World was certainly better than my mental image of tots showing up on MTV's *Spring Break Party and STD Fest* screaming "wooo-woooo!" for no apparent reason.

Having no idea that we were supposed to go to Disney World for spring break, I decided to salvage the situation by devising a week of "fun activities." On Day One, I spent four hours assembling a child-size pottery wheel before hurling the useless gizmo across the kitchen after realizing that a part was missing. Then it was off to the park, where I was overjoyed to see a mommy and daughter we knew playing together.

"Guess we're the only ones in town who didn't go to Disney World," I said brightly.

She hung her head. "We're leaving in the morning. Couldn't get a flight out until then."

Her tone was so serious that I had a flashback to those poor souls clinging to the helicopter skids during the fall of Saigon in 1975.

Sophie happily recited how she'd had a fun morning of watching mommy wrestle with the pottery-wheel-that-wasn't and screaming "Taiwanese piece of shit!" a lot.

It was a Kodak moment, I tell you.

On Day Two of our fun-filled Disney-less holiday, we decided to visit another park, one with a few more slides and swings.

"Wow! Now this is a park!" I said with much more enthusiasm than I felt. I tried not to pay attention to the fact that we were the only people there outside of a few home-schooled kids who, for reasons that I've never understood, insist on wearing long denim skirts everywhere they go.

Whew, I thought to myself. At first I thought the Rapture had come and we'd been overlooked, but I'm sure the homeschoolers would've made the cut.

"Isn't this great, honey?" I said in my best fake gush.

"At Disney World, they have a forty-foot-tall Pongo from *101 Dalmatians* and a swimming pool shaped like a grand piano *and* a waterslide where you spit right out of the sea serpent's mouth!" my daughter said.

"Oh, yeah? Well, over there is a fire ant hill. What do you want? Fantasy or real life?"

"I want the Seven Seas Lagoon and breakfast with Snow White and the Seven Dwarfs," she said.

"Not to worry. That guy sleeping on the bench over there looks a lot like Dopey."

Of course, after a couple of years of this, we realized there was no putting off our trip to Disney any longer.

We'd done rustic, noncommerical kinds of vacations (read: no cable) before, but I was sick of all the nature and lobsters that we found in our visits to a family cabin in Maine. I was craving total escape and plastic happiness, and no one delivers that like Disney.

Besides, I was getting a little burned out on lobster. The last time we'd gone to Maine (state motto: "The Prettiest Place on Earth for Maybe Forty-five to Sixty Days of the Year"), we went during the high season for lobsters.

Here's a typical restaurant experience in Maine.

ME: I'll have the fillet wrapped in bacon, and steamed broccoli for my side dish.

WAITRESS: I'm sorry. We're out of that. How about some delicious Maine lobster?

ME: Well, it is undeniably delicious, but I've eaten steamed lobster now three times a day for five days, and I'm fairly much over it. Do you have anything else?

WAITRESS: Sure we do! We have lobster salad, lobster rolls, and lobster bisque.

ME: No, no, I mean do you have any specials that don't involve lobster?

WAITRESS: This is Maine. Isn't this why you come up here? All the tourists love our lobsters and our delicious Maine syrup that we sell in overpriced bottles shaped just like maple leaves.

ME: Yes, they're charming. Okay, how about a sandwich for my kid? Maybe some peanut butter?

WAITRESS *(excited)*: With lobster jelly?

Suffice it to say, we were all ready for a change, and you

couldn't get further from the scenic beauty of Maine than Disney World, still beautiful in its own way.

So we did it! We bought plane tickets and even opted to stay at a hotel on-site, although Disney World's definition of *on-site* is rather generous. While technically still on Disney property, our, ahem, budget-priced Disney hotel was still a twenty-minute bus ride from everything.

My husband complained that "Next time, we're going to stay at one of the places on the monorail," and I explained that they cost five hundred dollars a night compared to our nifty sixty-eight dollars a night with tub faucets that let you twist Jimmy Neutron's head clean off if you want to. And I have always wanted to.

"Only the codgers stay in this place," I said, trying not to look wistful as we strolled across the shiny marble floors in the Grand Floridian's lobby.

There was no denying that boarding that bus every morning for our fourteen-hour day was getting a little old. Most of the time we managed to get seats, but this meant that the twenty or so left standing stuck their behinds in our faces. I pressed my head to the window and turned sideways, making myself flat as a flounder to avoid the dreaded face full of stranger ass.

On our first night at Disney, we surprised Sophie with late seating for Cinderella's Gala Feast, where you get to spend thirty-seven dollars for chicken fingers and buttered noodles shaped like Ariel the mermaid. It's worth it because Cinderella herself strolls from table to table posing for pictures and smiling demurely.

Thanks to a tip from a smart mommy friend of mine, I knew that Sophie would need to be dressed in full princess regalia: a poufy ice-blue Cinderella gown and coordinating "glass" slippers. Otherwise, we'd have been like the sad Ohio family with the screaming little girl: "Everybody else is dressed up. *I HATE YOU!*"

We spent the next three days getting up at dawn, wolfing microwaved pancakes shaped like Mickey's head at the "food" court, and queuing up for the bus that would take us to whatever magical adventure awaited.

At the end of our fourth fourteen-hour day in a row, I found myself standing under the big metallic golf ball thingy in Epcot, screaming to my husband: "If you don't let us rest, I'm going to kill you and then divorce you!"

"Fine, fine," he muttered absentmindedly while consulting his wrinkled park map. "You can rest while we board Spaceship Earth. By the way, did you know that Epcot stands for Experimental Prototype Community of Tomorrow?"

"We know, Daddy," said Soph.

He looked hurt.

Disney had turned my normally laid-back hubby into a goal-oriented nut job. On Day One, we visited Magic Kingdom and Epcot; Day Two was Animal Kingdom and back to Epcot; Day Three was MGM and, you guessed it, Epcot; Day Four was Magic Kingdom, Epcot, and Downtown Disney;

Day Five was Magic Kingdom until the flight home. Never have so few seen so much in such a short time.

I started to understand why so many people rent electric scooters to get through the park, although I grew to hate their irritated-sounding little horns as drivers tried to part the sea of tourists like Moses on a moped.

Disney inspires this sort of weird competitiveness. My husband took enormous pride in having us first in line every morning at the park of the day. He planned our stops with military precision, at one time warning us that we had "T minus three minutes to pee" or we'd miss Buzz Lightyear's Space Ranger Spin.

As we hurried out of yet another sparkling Disney restroom (these people descend on a gum wrapper like a SWAT team), I heard a little boy crying and watched his father get down on one knee to console him. "You know, son, you better tell me what the shit you're crying about, 'cause *you're the only reason we're here!*"

What can I tell you? Failure to get a Fastpass for Space Mountain can make a parent do crazy things.

As the week wore on, we became a Disney movie unto ourselves. *Honey, I Shrunk the Bank Account* opens with a tight shot of the three of us wolfing four-dollar hot dogs washed down with Cokes in twelve-dollar souvenir cups in Tomorrowland. I tried not to think about how much delicious Maine lobster that would have bought.

Is Disney expensive? Well, yes. Is it worth it? You bet your eleven-dollar fluorescent hot pink spring-loaded mouse ears it is.

Like any place that attracts kids, there were gift kiosks and shops everywhere. I had to admit it was all a lot more cheery than our last family trip, which had included a visit to the traveling *Titanic* exhibit. After a heartrending tour of the ship, you were dumped directly into a themed gift shop that sold glow-in-the-dark "icebergs" and even a foot-long replica of the *Titanic* made of milk chocolate. What kind of lesson was that? "Titanic: The Candy Bar That Hundreds Died For! Bite steerage in the morning and save first class for an afternoon snack!"

I saw plenty of Disney-philes push-pulling huge coolers full of snacks through the parks. I can't imagine going to the trouble, myself. There's sensible, and then there's just stupid-cheap. (Overheard in front of Mickey's PhilharMagic: "Sissie, it's you and Memaw's turn to watch the cooler.") You've already paid $150 for a four-day park pass, and you're quibbling over a sixteen-dollar lunch? Get over yourself.

A friend who always stays at the Disney campground (remember, Disney-style camping isn't exactly roughing it— they have their own *shows* and cabins with cable) told me she can fix dinner right there and save money on meals out. I told her I'd rather have a threesome with Chip 'n' Dale than cook on vacation, but to each her own.

By the end of the trip, Disney's merchandising magic had done its job: Sophie became obsessed with Pal Mickey, a "huggable, lovable interactive Theme Park tour guide." He's stuffed, stands about a foot tall, and costs $56.33. She tearfully begged for Pal Mickey, and we said no. It was silly, we thought, to buy a stuffed animal that yammered endlessly about park hours and attractions when we'd be home soon.

On our last day, as we boarded the very last bus that would take us back to the hotel before grabbing a cab to the airport, Sophie seemed to have moved past Pal Mickey. We had gone exactly one hour and thirty-five minutes without hearing about him. Home free, I thought.

There was only one seat left on the bus. Soph and I took it. And then I saw Pal Mickey grinning at us across the aisle. Soph started talking to his owner, who later became known as "You know, the little girl whose parents really *do* love her."

The little girl's parents, who were wearing matching XXL Donald Duck sweatshirts and fanny packs emblazoned with all seven dwarfs, glared at my husband and me as if we should be reported to Child Protective Services.

I could read their minds: *Cheap jerks. Buy the kid Pal Mickey.* And I hoped they couldn't read mine: *Y'all are really fat.*

The truth is, everybody at Disney World is fat. If you're not fat when you go, you're fat coming out. I walked fourteen miles a day and couldn't zip my jeans by the end of the trip. Go figure.

I think it's something in the hot dogs.

2

Yo Yo Yo! Where Can a Sista Get a Cowgirl Outfit?

Holidays Make This Mama Wanna Get in Your Grille

So, it's practically Valentine's Day, and I've found myself paying special attention to how the kindergarten set deals with affairs of the heart.

"Valentimes," as my kindergartener explained it, is a very big deal. It's truly the sweetest age, the last year when little boys will skip together while holding hands and not think twice about it.

Thankfully, there have been some improvements to the old Valentine system I remember from grade school, when the not-so-popular kids got five or six valentines and everybody else got a whole bunch. It was a hateful little ritual that nobody seemed to notice was slap-your-baby cruel.

Now, because we have Oprah, we're a little more aware of how this sort of dissing can not only damage self-esteem but also lead to a life of crime or sitcom writing. So notes are sent home saying that "Valentines should be given to every child in the class, not just the cute, rich, and smart ones." (Well, that was the gist of it.)

The girls, as you might expect, seem to be ahead of the game on things romantic. They prefer to play house during recess with designated "mommy," "daddy," and "baby" instead of the boys' favorite, some sort of army-man, video-game soldier thing that involves lots of running around for no reason and screaming *"You're my prisoner!"* to the pampas grass.

Not long ago, my daughter confided that one of the little boys in her class had threatened to kiss her on the playground. Apparently a romantic subplot had developed among the soldiers.

Because hubby and I are basically nerds, we considered this a "teachable moment" and launched a loving but firm and very PC lecture about not allowing anyone to do anything to you that you don't like.

But then the truth came out.

"Well," she said, "he didn't really want to that much, but all of us girls chased him and finally caught him and he said he'd kiss us if we didn't let him go."

Ah, well, then. Carry on, soldiers. War does strange things to a man's brain, I guess.

With so much romance in the air, the princess has been thinking about her own marital future. "I don't think I'm going to get married until I'm *fifteen,*" she announced at the dinner table one night.

Well, that's a relief. We were afraid she was going to do something crazy.

"Where on earth will you live?" I asked.

"Well, here, of course," she said. And the groom? "Well, he'll have to go live with his mommy and daddy. After he gets a job and buys me some stuff."

Okay, this might work out after all.

While Valentine's Day is a favorite holiday around our house (how can anything dedicated to chocolate be bad?), it's not as much fun as Halloween.

This year, we decided that the princess would be a cowgirl. It was so fabulously retro, I decided. You know. Fringed suede vest, maybe a ruffly denim skirt, red bandanna, hat, boots, and a little six-shooter.

Easy enough, I thought.

Because I am famously incapable of sewing (having sewn the pockets onto the inside of my final-exam apron back in seventh grade home ec class), it was going to have to be store-bought.

Our first stop was a famous toy store that has a backwards *R* in the middle.

"Where are your six-shooters, hon?" I asked the earnest-faced young man standing in the weapons aisle.

"Huh?"

"Toy pistols, hon. You know, maybe a couple of them

with a holster so Missy Poo here can be a proper cowgirl for Halloween."

He looked at me with disdain. "We don't carry guns here."

"No, of course you don't," I said. "I want a *toy* gun. I'm sure y'all have those here at We Be Toys, don't you?"

"No guns!" he kind of shrieked. The princess and I looked at each other, puzzled.

I tried logic. "But you've got machetes, tanks, and missile launchers right here," I said. "What's the big deal?"

"No guns!"

"Okay," I said, using my best hostage-negotiator-calm voice. "I got the whole guns-kill-people thing, but what do you think is on the front of that huge green regulation army tank on the shelf behind you? Are those babies going to fire chocolate frosting onto the enemy? I think not."

For reasons that I don't come close to understanding, I have noticed that, the older I get, the more often I am prone to lapse into a pathetic middle-aged-white-woman attempt at rapper cool when extremely frustrated.

The first time it happened was when my cable went out and, therefore, my Internet connection. I had spent the whole day home alone with an inability to Google myself. Yes, I know it sounds nasty, but it's more fun than a big bowl of meth. Kidding!

Anywho, I heard myself tell the nice cable man, "Listen

bruh, you better MacGyver something quick, cuz I'm jonesin' for my broadband."

So, it was happening again in the toy store. Frustration leads to rap in me. Fo' shizzle.

I eyed the sales boy. "Don't you see, er, home slice, it's the same thing? Except we want a six-shooter."

"Look, it's store policy not to carry them," my vested friend said, hoping that someone, anyone, would page him. And soon.

"I feel ya, my face gator," I said, again lapsing into this curious rapspeak and wondering why, even as I was saying it. "But I just want to make a point here. . . . I mean I'm up in here with my girl. I'm in the house and I got the Benjamins, so whassup?"

Alas, we finally accepted defeat, but only after I'd, I think, flashed some gang signs and announced "It's all good" to no one in particular.

We got back into my ghetto sled and moved on to search for the costume components. Six stores and endless rap frustration later, the closest we'd come was something called Diva Cowgirl! It was a hideous hot pink shiny metallic skirt with a fringy top. Frankly, it looked like it would have been more at home in an Old West brothel, worn by one of those hoochie mamas you always saw hugging the bar at Miss Kitty's saloon on *Gunsmoke*.

Once again, I silently cursed the fact that I was a craft feeb.

Across town, my friend was busily stitching a VW Beetle costume, complete with working windshield wipers for her daughter.

Bitch.

We even stopped at the fabric store, where I thought I could buy some cow-print fabric and cut a little vest out.

"Mommy, what are you *doing?*" asked my daughter, horrified.

"It's a pattern. Mommy can use this to make your Halloween costume. How hard can it be to make a vest?"

"Have you been drinking?"

Whoa. That hurt. Although it was a perfectly reasonable question.

That night, I discovered everything I wanted on eBay, the catch being that it would cost $150 or, with shipping, about $386.

The white sheet with cut-out eyeholes was starting to look really good.

But not good enough for the princess, who ended up borrowing a fabulous real suede cowgirl outfit from my friend Amy, who always comes through in a pinch.

Amy's one of those friends who is relentlessly prepared for everything. So, in less time than it took for me to transform into Gangsta Mama, I had everything we needed, including a tiny little pearl revolver and matching holster.

We loved the cowgirl outfit so much that it became that year's Christmas card.

My friend Mona, whose kid is not allowed to play with guns and therefore spends all day fashioning Uzis from bent pecan tree limbs, was horrified.

"Is that a gun in that holster?" she asked, incredulous.

"Well, hell yeah, Mona. She'd look pretty goofy wearing an empty holster, now, wouldn't she?"

"You shouldn't encourage that sort of thing," she said while I watched her son turn a magnolia seedpod into an amazingly realistic grenade.

"Fire in the hole, y'all!" he hollered.

Once we got past the horrors of Halloween, there was scarcely time to take a breath before it was time for the annual Freeze Your Ass Off Fall Festival Fund-raiser at school.

If you have a kid in elementary school, you know all about the Fall Festival, which is held to celebrate the old-time notion of "harvest." This is a cute idea, I guess, but if you think about it, it's not like any of these kids has brought in a crop or will ever contemplate going to the barn dance with a gal named Millie.

It is, however, an excuse to have fun and raise a little money, usually for the PTA, which I most certainly believe in and would never, ever say anything against on account of these people have more power in their pinkie toenail than I will ever have in my whole pathetic life. So, go PTA!

The Fall Festival, then, isn't about celebrating a bounteous harvest. No, no. It is about finding the one dummy in the planning session who says, "Sure! I'll run the popcorn concession."

Looking back on it, I was actually smug about my assignment. Let the rest of them run the bingo, the salmonella—er, petting zoo—or the thing I did last year: the throw-the-beanbag-through-the clown's-eyes until you either win a prize or burst into tears and scream *"Mean lady!"* and get *two* prizes and all the change in the mean lady's pockets.

The popcorn concession, as it turned out, was a two-foot-tall glass box that said *Hot Popcorn* on it in happy red script. It was stashed on the floor of a broom closet and weighed approximately eighteen hundred pounds.

After a few minutes of huffing and puffing, I found Hans and Franz to help me tote the thing across the playground.

Okay, I said, looking at the empty glass box, *start popping!* After a few wretched moments, I realized this was no microwave but rather some sort of Amish popcorn concession that used—get this—oil and actual popcorn kernels.

All alone at my post and surrounded by freckle-faced accusers who wanted to know when the popcorn would be ready, I decided to read the directions. Turns out you had to heat the thing for eight minutes. Next, you had to measure oil into the basket gizmo. Then (and here's the tricky part) while the blasted thing rotated with tiny blades that stir the kernels, you had to dodge the blades to continually add kernels.

It was then that I realized that the proper name for this

particular corner of Fall Festival hell was Let's Visit the Whirling Popcorn Machine of Death.

Burn, spatter, dodge, weave.

I finally managed to make my first sale, and the kid complained that the popcorn was burned.

"Yeah? Well, so am I. Get used to it."

He looked hurt.

"Oh, all right. And here's all the change in my pockets."

We'd barely had time to take a breath after all the "fun" of the Fall Festival when my daughter announced plans for Thanksgiving.

As she sat in the backseat on the way to school, she solemnly examined her cuter-'n'-hell hot pink velour pantsuit.

"What's wrong, pumpkin?" I said cheerily after seeing a definite frowny face in my rearview window.

"We were *supposed* to wear black dresses so we could be pilgrims today," she said petulantly.

"Huh?" I asked, mildly irritated that the Allman Brothers classic "Blue Sky" had just come on the radio and, instead of listening to it, I must now discover that, through no fault of my own, I was pilgrim-deficient.

"You know, Mommy, for the Thanksgiving feast. You're making the mashed potatoes and it's at nine thirty and all the other mommies are going to be there and one of them's even going to make *gravy!*"

Okay, that hurts. Every kid in the neighborhood knows

that I make the worst gravy in seven states. It is notoriously thin and flavorless and is eventually tossed with great drama and some few tears onto the backs of lingering yard cats every danged Thanksgiving afternoon.

"Whoa," I said, while the Brothers crooned about blue skies and sunny days and Lord knows what they'll do if she takes her love away.

"Okay," I said as calmly as possible. "A costume? You're supposed to wear a costume?"

"Well, just a black dress, kind of pouffy, you know, like the Pilgrims wore to eat with the Native Americans."

"Indians," I growled.

"Mommy!"

Oh, spare me a PC grade-schooler. And why had I picked this morning to give up caffeine? Why hadn't I given up, I dunno, maize instead?

"Honey," I said, "why didn't you tell me about this last week? You know Mommy needs a little more than (looks at watch), hmmm, thirty-six seconds' notice."

"There was a note in my backpack. Didn't you read it?"

Busted. Okay, I admit it. There are so *many* notes that I may have missed a few. Late library books, homework sheets, Picasso-like artwork—I tell you, hons, some days I expect to pull a live squirrel monkey out of that thing.

OKAY, DO NOT PANIC, I thought. I thought it just like that, in capital letters. There was still, after all, twenty-two seconds to return home and throw on the most somber and Pilgrim-like dress she had, and that's what we did.

"Thee looks beautiful," I said as we raced into the school, a ten-pound bag of potatoes slapping against my sweat-pants.

"Thanks, Mommy," she said with a bright smile. "Oh, and Mommy, don't forget, I said you'd make the corny-copia."

Thee is *so* grounded.

3

Stop Dressing Your Six-Year-Old Like a Skank

The princess had just graduated to a size 7 when everything went to shit. We headed for our favorite department store, ready to take that leap into the new world of 7–16. Bye-bye, 4–6X, I thought to myself with a tug of sadness. My baby was growing up.

And apparently into a prostitute.

"Where are the sevens?" I asked the sixty-something clerk who wore her glasses on a chain just like me.

"You're standing in 'em," she said.

Oh, no, I thought, looking around. *Oh no, no, no, no, no, no.*

"There must be some mistake," I said. "These are, well, slutty-looking. I'm talking about clothes for a little girl in first grade."

"That's all we got."

"But these look like things *a hooker would wear!*"

She smiled sadly. "You have no idea how many times I hear that every day."

Okay, breathe. This is just some weird marketing experiment. Right?

I went to my second-favorite department store and was invited to peruse the awfulness that is Tweenland! A better name would be Lil Skanks!

Sequins, fringe, neon glitter tank tops with big red lips on them, fishnet sleeves, scary dragon faces lunging from off-the-shoulder T-shirts. Whither the adorable seersucker? The pastel floral short sets? The soft cotton dresses in little-girl colors like lavender, pale pink, periwinkle blue? This stuff practically screamed SYRINGE SOLD SEPARATELY.

I get it. Now that my kid is practically of childbearing age (is six the new seventeen?) I must choose from ripped-on-purpose jeans and T-shirts that scream things like BABY DOLL and JAIL BAIT, not to mention a rather angry GIRLS *RULE* AND BOYS *DROOL!* where an embroidered flower with buzzing bee should be.

When did this happen? Who decided that my six-year-old should dress like a Vegas showgirl? And one with an abundance of anger issues at that?

And why are parents buying this junk fashioned from cheesy fabrics that surely leave your dryer's lint filter full of glitter and fuzzy sequined balls?

I hope you won't take this the wrong way—you, the mom

on the cell phone flipping your check card to your kid so she can buy the jeans that say SPANK ME on them—but you're going down, bitch.

No, really. I'm taking you out, putting you on notice, slapping some sense into your sorry ass.

Just for old times' sake, I wandered through the 4–6X section. It was just an arm's length away, but it was the difference between a Happy Meal at the playground and bulimia at the bar. So far, these clothes had been left mercifully untouched by the wand of the skank fairy, whom I envision as looking a lot like Tara Reid.

Instead of being able to buy pretty things for my daughter, sweet somethings in ice cream colors, I must now shop at big, boxy unisex stores where you can still buy shorts that don't say DELICIOUS on the bottom or T-shirts that are plain instead of, swear to God, a size 7 belly shirt with MADE YA LOOK on the front. Look at what? There's not supposed to be anything to look at on a seven-year-old. *Because they're children.*

Sweet Jesus, what I'd do for a lousy ladybug collar on a smocked dress. Instead, this season's Easter look consisted of sequined and chiffon body-hugging sheaths.

I know that my daughter and I will fight about clothes in a few years, perhaps horribly, but, for now, there will be none of this Little Ladies of the Night look.

And while moms and daughters have always fought over clothes (let's face it, even Marcia Brady wore some shockingly short dresses, and those baby-doll pj's in front of stepbrother Greg were icky), the clothing wars were usually taking place between mom and teen, not mom and first-grader.

When you see a size 7 shirt that says SEXY! or a mom and her little girl strolling through the mall in matching shorts with JUICY scrawled across the butt, you have to wonder what the hell is going on.

The saddest part about all this is that if you dress like you're a twenty-two-year-old going out to a club after a tough day at work in the city, you don't get to enjoy being a little kid.

Deliver me from an outraged third-grader who thinks she's entitled to the entire line at Abercrombie & Fitch. Put on a normal pair of jeans and go play kickball, you brat! And tell yo mama I said so.

If you examine the offerings in the 7–16 department, you'll quickly discover that it's no different from the stuff in the juniors' department and beyond. There is no distinction between a kid in second grade and one in twelfth grade and a college grad who's started her first real job. Never mind how essentially stupid a little fifty-pound kid looks wearing an off-the-shoulder top with FOOL FOR LOVE in glitter letters. Hell, some of these kids can't even read cursive writing and they're wearing this junk. They adore it because it's what Gwen or Avril or Ashlee is wearing. *But you're not on stage,* I want to scream. *You're on the monkey bars!*

The big difference between my childhood and my daughter's is that these days, the kid gets the final say. What's up with that? I can promise you that if I was eight years old and told my parents I needed eighty-dollars for sparkly jeans to rest on my hip bones and a midriff top that read TOO RICH FOR YOU, they'd have thought I had fallen off my bike and my brain had spilled out my ears.

If you want to get at the heart of the problem, which is the parents, of course, you need look no further than those "nanny to the rescue" shows on TV.

It's the oddest thing: In almost every show, the moms are spilling out of too-tight tank tops and Daisy Dukes. They look like teenagers, and the kids run all over them.

When the sturdy, bespectacled Supernanny shows up at the jam-stained front door, it's clear that a new sheriff is in town. The kids see her as someone they should probably listen to. Hmmm. Wonder if that has anything to do with the fact that she's not wearing a tank that says SWEET THANG. She means business, while Mama's over there cowering in the kitchen corner, all hair extensions and implants talking 'bout "I can't do a thing with these young'uns."

These children should be thanking the TV gods that they didn't dispatch a tough-talking Southern bubba instead of the Supernanny. Bubba doesn't care about any Dr. Phil–ish reasons for misbehavior. He'd just arrange for "a date with Mr. Hickory Stick" and a dessert of Dial soap while saying things like, "I'll learn you some respect, lil tater."

Okay, that's going too far, but you get the idea. I always preferred the count-to-three method of discipline. It was astonishingly effective. You want to take back parental power? Try saying "Onnnne," then "Twooooo." I never made it to "Threeeee," because my preschooler shaped up, for which I am eternally grateful, because, let's face it, if I ever got to three, I had nothing. Nada. Zip.

If you ask me, the Supernanny should put the parents, not the kids, in the naughty room and not let them out until Mom promises to buy some clothes that fit and Dad can stop being such a wimp. ("Brandon calls his Mama names, and I just wanna cry!") Grow a spine, you freak. It's time to "man up"!

They're kids, not short grown-ups. Remember?

4

Flower (Girl) Power

We've Got the Dress—
Just Let Us Know When and Where

While attending the sixth wedding of the summer (doesn't anybody live in sin anymore?), my daughter once again looked longingly at the flower girl floating down the aisle to "Taco Bell's Canon," as she calls it.

The little girl scattered petals from a white wicker basket, her moiré taffeta skirt swishing noisily past us, her tulle hair bow taunting us.

"Why won't anybody ask me to be a flower girl?" Soph wailed.

"Oh, sweetie, being a flower girl isn't a big deal," I said. "It's just a few moments of glory, a gorgeous new outfit, a fancy hairstyle, and listening to a bunch of strangers tell you how beautiful you are when it's over. Rather like an episode of *Queer Eye for the Straight Guy*."

"Huh?"

"Never mind, sugar lump. I'm sure your time will come."

At that moment, her little friend piped up behind us, "I'm going to be a flower girl for the *third time* next month and I'm going to get my hair curled on top of my head and I'm going to look just like Cindy-rella. You've *never* been a flower girl?" She tossed back her head and laughed, then formed the dreaded *L* with her pudgy little nail-bitten fingers, identifying my precious as a "loser."

"That's okay," I said, a trifle too loudly. "She's just acting mean because she knows that her parents don't love her as much as her little sister."

"Waahhh!"

After this unpleasantness, I decided to put the word out that I had a flower girl for hire. We even had a dress. Last spring, when a friend postponed her wedding indefinitely on account of her fiancé lost his life's savings on one of those gambling cruise boats, we found ourselves stuck with a tastefully simple white organza dress with tiny yellow daisies dancing across the empire waist.

I told everyone that Sophie was ready to be a flower girl, and I was past the point of caring if it was for anyone we even knew. I knew she'd be great at it, not melting down like the really young ones. I hate it when people put their toddlers in weddings and end up pushing them down the aisle. It's not like we don't see all this, and it detracts from the sacredness of the moment to see the fat bottom of some woman in a silk shantung suit duck-walking down the aisle going, "Go on now, Misty Rae! You can do it!" Inevitably this is greeted with tears, and the flower basket is tossed until the duck-mama gives up and says loud enough for everyone to hear, "If you want that Dora's Talking Doll House, you'll move your ass down that aisle right now, little missy, you hear me?"

My daughter wouldn't even need to eat your reception food. Unless you were actually planning to serve Rugrats apple sauce and PB&J without the crusts, of course, which she would be powerless to resist.

And I'd make sure she stayed away from that nasty chocolate fountain that everybody's so crazy about now. I went to a wedding reception, and there was a little boy sticking his finger in the fountain, licking it down to his knuckle and then *sticking it back into the fountain*. It's not just kids, of course. Grown-ups act like idiots when they get around a chocolate fountain, oohing and aahing and *double-dipping* their half-eaten wedges of pound cake and strawberries, spreading their germs everywhere. And there's always that one redneck who thinks it's hilarious to stick his head in the fountain and let the chocolate drip down his throat. I swear, we near 'bout got divorced over that one.

The point is, my kid deserved to be a flower girl, and so, amazingly, she finally got her chance when my husband's sister, Linda, got married for the first time at age fifty-one.

We were thrilled for Linda and Todd because they seemed so well-suited for one another but, to be honest, I was even more thrilled that Sophie would finally get to be a flower girl. Unless . . .

What if Linda decided that she wanted a simple ceremony without any attendants whatsoever? I adore my sister-in-law, but she's a threat to go all intellectual-hippie on me at any given time. To be fair, when a woman has waited fifty-one years to marry the man of her dreams, she has every right to have the wedding she wants. Unless I decide otherwise.

I decided to give her a long-distance call.

"Linda, if you don't ask Sophie to be your flower girl, I swear that I will never speak to you again as long as I live."

"What are you talking about?" Linda said, genuinely puzzled. "Of course I want her to be my flower girl. I wouldn't have it any other way."

Oh, thank God! I had lost enough sleep over this. Sophie and I went shopping for the perfect flower girl dress (the one with the daisies was too small by now) and counted down the days to the big event.

Todd and Linda decided to incorporate some rituals from his Native American heritage into their wedding ceremony. Before the service began, they had a friend set some sage on fire and "smudge" the sanctuary of the church to purify it.

This was lovely and quite meaningful to everyone except for the late-arriving Aunt Tiny and Uncle Dink.

While a nephew home from college for the festivities optimistically noted that "Cool, this church smells like pot," Uncle Dink noisily shuffled from corner to corner, sniffing for the source of the "fire."

I suppose it's true that once a volunteer fireman, always a volunteer fireman, because even as Sophie walked into the church in her first-ever flower girl outfit, back straight, hair festooned with tiny white flowers, shy smile in place, Uncle Dink was swatting at the air in front of her. "The whole damn church is going to be on fire and nobody seems to give a damn. It's the damndest thing I've ever seen," he said, finally settling back into his rightful spot beside Aunt Tiny.

All we could think was, *Damn*.

I discreetly pulled Uncle Dink aside and told him that nothing was on fire, that it was just a purification ritual that involved burning sage. He looked relieved, but the nephew looked crestfallen.

"Oh, for God's sake," I hissed at him. "Did you think we were going to hand out big fat doobies like little bubble soap containers?"

He hung his head.

The wedding was beautiful, and the best part was seeing the flower girl proudly posing for pictures beside her beloved aunt after the ceremony.

Sophie had not only been a flower girl at last, but she had done it for someone she genuinely loved, not just some random couple that broke up because the groom-to-be couldn't stay away from the Lucky Lady Floating Casino and Hot Wings Bar.

Oh, and the second-best part? There wasn't a chocolate fountain in sight.

5

Weary Mom to Uppity Teens

At Least We Know Where the Continent of Chile Is

There's a great brouhaha brewing over the problem of poor writing among America's high school and college students.

Ain't hardly none of 'em can do it right, studies say.

Some blame the text messaging craze favored by the phone-as-umbilicus set. We've become a nation of instant messagers that has far surpassed the shorthand of my high school yearbook (motto: "not badly writ"), the uninspired 2 Sweet 2 B 4 gotten. That's right: I used 2B sweet.

As long as there've been parents and kids, the older has whined about how the younger can't write, spell, speak to elders, make fire, and so forth as good as they could at that age.

I think that instead of pointing fingers, we should help convince America's young people of the lifelong benefits of learning to write with thoughtful expression, correct grammar, and, of course, appropriate sin tax.

We should get back to basics in the classroom, teaching that conjugation isn't just something your redneck cousin wants to do when his girlfriend visits him in prison.

He hadn't oughta stole that man's bling, nohow.

According to members of the prestigious National Commission on Writing for America's Families, Schools, and Colleges (or "the Hulk" as they like to call themselves), even the English classes don't require much writing these days. And yonder lies the problem.

When I was in high school, we were not only required to read such literary masterpieces as *Beowulf* and *The Canterbury Tales,* which I believe were both written by J. K. Rowling, but we were also required to write ten-page reports about them. And while this assignment was as painful as an Arsenio comeback, there's no doubt that it built character and made my writing gooder than it had been before.

Today's students, say the Hulk, don't know that you shouldn't never end a sentence with a preposition. A way we used to remember this was to gently correct "Where you at?" with "Behind the preposition at." Hey, this is what passed for snappy rejoinder back in the day. It would also get us beat up if said to the wrong person. ("Now where you at? On the ground, that's where!")

The most important advice the experts have is to get kids to start reading more. I believe it's already working. Just last week, I saw at least a half dozen sunscreened nine-year-olds sitting around a pool reading the latest Harry Potter book.

While their parents pleaded with them to come swim, they waved them away without even looking up except to ask them please not to splash page 4,016 again.

So as you can see, there's lots of hope for a new generation of great writers.

The hope dwindles as the little puddin's get older, though. In a recent survey, more U.S. teens could name the Three Stooges than the three branches of the federal government, which, as those of us old enough to recall high school civics classes know to be the the legislative, the executive, and the Moe.

It's very trendy to whine about how little our young adults know about government. How many times have we seen teens draw a blank when asked to name this great nation's vice president or, for that matter, the prime minister of Kansas?

Teens today are not dumb. Quite the contrary. They have even invented their own language, an abbreviated sort of speech that allows them to chat back and forth on their cell phones using symbols and letters that cannot be deciphered by anyone old enough to remember mood rings.

Thus, *I'm looking forward to seeing you again soon* (which, now that I write it, has all the appeal of sitting in the parlor and listening to 78s on the family Victrola) becomes simply *ltr*.

I'm not so sure this is a gd thg. Still, you must applaud today's young people for their technological savvy. Most can download an entire library of music in less time than it takes me to pit my prunes.

I believe we will see a nation in which Speaker of the House Jack Osbourne will say, "All we want is some frickin' respect. Buttholes."

But, dear Jack, respect must be earned. Those who refuse to remember the mistakes of the past are doomed to end up on shows like *I'm a Celebrity—Get Me Outta Here!*

What I'm saying is that it's possible to be cool and to know a little bit about history. If you ask a teen today to locate Vietnam on a map, there is not a doubt in my mind that he will say, "I dunno, dawg, but I'm pretty sure it's one of the blue ones."

Young people today have an abysmal knowledge of geography. They can't recall the names of the continents (and, hey, nobody's perfect—I almost always forget Chile).

So what's the solution to a nation filled with young people who honestly believe that Springfield is home to Bart Simpson, not Abraham Lincoln?

The return of civics classes (which, by law, must be taught by the same guy who teaches driver's ed *and* dates the homely but kind school librarian)?

Mayhaps. Otherwise, and I hate to say this, we may be looking at a future that includes two words that should never, ever be put together: President Britney.

While it's easy to act as if we grown-ups have all the answers, we don't. Witness what happened when I tried to help my second-grader with a science project.

Scrambling into the backseat of the car at the end of school, she paused long enough to look me in the eye. Was that disgust I saw in the eyes of my precious?

"You're fired!" she growled with a dismissive flick of her hand. All that was missing was the famous Trump hair turban.

Okay, so I "helped" her with a couple of school projects and they didn't go so well. It was late, the project was overdue, and who really cares if a sea turtle is a mammal or a rodent or whatever, anyway?

Here's a flash: They're not mammals. Not even close. But they come under the heading of "sea creatures," so that was good enough for me. While other, smarter mommies had assisted in constructing dioramas of rain forests, working volcanoes, and battery-operated solar systems, we chose a mammals-from-the-sea theme housed in a shell-lined shoe-box. Which would've been killer if we had left out the turtle. This, coupled with my "help" on two math homework problems that turned out to be wrong, resulted in my firing.

Of course, I know that turtles aren't mammals. They are ambivalents, which can live on air or underwater and write with their right or left flippers. They also almost never vote.

Although the science project ended poorly, it wasn't a waste of time, because we also got to learn about the dwarf sea horse. These tiny creatures have a colt's head, a monkey's tail, and a chameleon's independently roving eyes. ("You talking to me? *You talking to me?* Oh, I give up.")

While all that is fascinating, the coolest thing we learned is that the dwarf sea horse doesn't have a stomach. That's right! It has what is called "a continuous gut." This anomaly is only found in the Florida Keys and, occasionally, the nation's finer Golden Corral restaurants.

The dwarf sea horse searches constantly for food, all day and into the night. Although I don't have the head of a colt, I must have some dwarf sea horse in me.

Another cool thing we learned about these weird little creatures is that the male gives birth. That's right! The female, who is desperately out there trying to find a late-night drive-through, deposits the eggs in the male's pouch, and he takes care of them, presumably giving up caffeine and highlights just to be on the safe side.

Studies have shown that although the males carry the babies, they actually invest about half as much metabolic energy as females do in producing offspring. Everybody say duh-huh.

So, in conclusion, turtles are not mammals, Donald Trump is a mammal but not warm-blooded, and I am, at least in the eyes of one elementary school student, toast.

6

Hilary Duff & Us

When Motherhood Hits Those Inevitable Valleys, We'll Always Have "the Hils"

Hons, I am finally a hero in my daughter's eyes. Not because I snatched her from the jaws of a rabid dingo or plucked her from a deadly riptide. No, no. I'm a real hero because I have secured tickets to the Hilary Duff concert.

To those of you who don't know Hilary Duff from Howard Duff, this is a Very Big Deal. It's like if you were a parent back in '64 and came home one day waving tickets to *The Ed Sullivan Show* and asking, "Hey! Who'd like to see four mop-topped cuties from Liverpool perform tonight?"

Hilary is a squeaky-clean teen queen with a passable voice who plays to sold-out audiences of "tweens." My daughter and her best friend adore Hilary. They sleep in Lizzie McGuire nightgowns (Hilary's TV show character—try to hang here, will you?), they wear Lizzie tennis shoes, they carry Lizzie purses.

As role models go, Hilary's okay. There was that reported flap between her and the tiresomely tough Avril Lavigne (Hil said Avril didn't appreciate her fans enough—sigh) and a spat with Lindsay Lohan at the *Freaky Friday* premiere (Hil stole her boyfriend, hunkette Aaron Carter), but generally, she's no diva. I know it's true 'cause I read it in *Bop* magazine.

At forty-seven, I knew I'd probably be the oldest mom in the Bi-Lo Center in Greenville, South Carolina, and even as the tears of joy spilled like tiny diamonds down my precious daughter's cheeks, she managed to choke out, "Uh, can you maybe sit behind us or maybe somewhere in the back?"

Ouch.

Just for that, my friend and I intend to do as our foremothers did before us and embarrass the dookie out of our little girls. I'm going to jump up and down and make those hand signals that the kids all make, the ones that I'm not sure whether they're gang signs or mean *I love you* in Hawaiian. I'm going to sing along to all of Hilary's songs, wear a belly shirt that says MRS. TIMBERLAKE, and get something unprintable pierced.

Although I'm whining a bit about the long drive, the high ticket prices, the inevitable purchase from the Duff Stuff kiosk, and so forth, I'm actually pretty excited.

Your first concert is something you never forget, and I'll be right there, in Section 6, Row D, to see my baby's reaction. I got a little misty recounting to her my first time: a two-hour trip to see Humble Pie and King Crimson with my sorta-boyfriend's kindly daddy driving six of us and waiting in the parking lot for three hours.

"He was a hero just like you, Mom," she said.

Word.

Fast-forward a few weeks, and there I am, crouching behind the wheel well of Hilary Duff's tour bus. It's so big and gorgeous that it brings tears to my eyes.

From a distance, I must've looked like the world's oldest tween queen stalker. Not like that crazy-eyed one who just got arrested for harassing Catherine Zeta-Jones because Michael Douglas is her soul mate, but a kinder, gentler stalker who just wants a cool picture for her kid.

As I stood with my friend and our daughters on a sweltering sidewalk in Greenville, six hours from home, I wondered aloud if we should hang out in the lobby at the Hyatt in case "the Hils" was staying there. We'd heard that earlier in the day in the breakfast buffet, and I'd immediately lost my appetite and started squealing and flapping.

Duff stalkers were everywhere that day. It's just that most of them were size 0 and looked eerily like Duff herself. I, on the other hand, was wearing my official Mommy big-shorts, the khaki ones that make my ass look eight ax-handles across, and carrying two cameras and a camcorder, just in case. I was also seized with an irrational urge to tell every kid walking by to "stand up straight, and get your damn bangs out of your eyes." The world's oldest and most uncool Duff stalker.

Sophie's friend Emeline had won backstage passes to meet Hilary, so we were feeling pretty smug as we walked from our hotel to the arena, where we saw many thousands of other little girls dressed in short pleated skirts, jeans jackets, and hair adornments, most trailed by tired moms.

We were whisked to the side with the other "meet and greet" winners—an intimate gathering of about two hundred, as it turned out—and escorted to the rear of the convention center, where we passed roadies cooking hamburgers. Someone squealed at the sight of an enormous suds-filled washing machine: "I'll bet Hilary's clothes are *in there!*" Sophie said I was embarrassing her. Well. It *could've* been her clothes.

When Hilary appeared from behind a blue curtain, well, I 'bout died. I have met the Queen of England and Dan Aykroyd in my day. Once, Melanie Griffith filmed a movie right across the street from my house, and I found Antonio Banderas standing on my very own sidewalk. And, yes, it's true, he's really short, but it didn't matter because how many times are you going to walk out to your car and go, "Oh, hi, Antonio!" and have him smile back and wave. I tell you this so you don't think I'm like some hick who's never seen a celebrity up close and personal.

And here stood Hilary Duff, way tinier than she looks on TV.

We got pictures of Sophie and Emeline with Hilary before being shooed out by a very large bodyguard. The concert was fun. At sixteen, Hilary was all high-energy pop/rock without a hint of naisty. There was something unexpectedly touching about all those little girls sitting beside their mommies, singing all the words of all the songs together.

I wanted to hold on to the moment because I know that the future holds awful arguments about dates, driving privileges, and general distrust. But like every other mom at that concert who found herself holding up a glow-stick instead of a Bic lighter, I know that there's a good chance that it will be healed just a little when we turn to each other and say, "Remember the time we met Hilary Duff?"

7

Field Trips, Fornification, and a Shit-Eating Giraffe

Who Says School Can't Be Fun?

School field trips to celebrate the end of the school year are better than I remember. My daughter's recent trip to the zoo sure topped my own memory of a two-hour bus ride to the maximum-security Central Prison in Raleigh, North Carolina, where we were given a less-than-PC tour. ("Now over here, you got yer crazy-eyed serial killers. . . . Over yonder, you got yer habitual fornificators.")

I'm fairly confident that the reason crime is on the increase is that nobody takes those field trips anymore. That's why you have your fornificating going on right and left.

The annual field trip to prison had the desired effect, which was to scare the livin' crap out of every little Southern boy and girl so that they would never go astray. It worked, too. To my knowledge, not a single kid in my fifth-grade class ever pursued a life of crime, and I can tell you it's because none of us ever truly recovered from seeing those prisoners waving good-bye, tattooed arms stretching through the bars, giving us the finger.

I realize now that having hundreds of North Carolina school children file by and gawk at you is a violation of all kinds of prisoner privacy and personal rights and so on, but bottom line, we were so scared after that ritual, we just wanted to go home and hug our mamas and never so much as jaywalk.

It was an incredibly effective deterrent but not the sort of thing you can do today with entire busloads of children. A parent today could sue, claiming that their kid was posttraumatic-stressed by the whole thing.

It would be cheaper and just as effective to force school kids to watch every season of HBO's *Oz* on DVD.

After a few hours of seeing what can happen if you get the wrong cellmate (the creepy white supremacist who makes you wear mascara and lipstick, for example), you'd be scared straight, all right.

Of course, the prison field trip wasn't the only one we took. There was the annual trek to the local wastewater treatment facility, or as we called it, "the dookie factory."

Sure, it was a small school in a poor, rural county, a hundred miles from, well, anywhere. It wasn't exactly like we could dash over to MoMA for the Diane Arbus retrospective, so we had to make do with what we had.

Still, it's hard to imagine why anyone thought it was a good idea to give sewage plant tours to snickering adolescents. The highlight was observing the trap that catches the condoms.

A lot of colors and styles were evident, which made us all look at our boring little town in a whole new light. Apparently, there was a steamy side to life out there beyond the rows of corn, tomatoes, and soybeans.

A lot of people were gettin' some. Maybe more than some.

Big Eugene, who could usually be found smoking beneath the pecan trees on the schoolyard while the rest of us in fifth grade played hopscotch, announced that the wilder condoms were something called "French ticklers." We said, "I know *that*," but Big Eugene, who had flunked an ungodly number of grades and already had a pencil-thin mustache, merely scowled dismissively at us through the haze from his Benson & Hedges. He knew we were lying, and even though we knew deep in our hearts that one day Big Eugene would be flipping off schoolchildren from his jailhouse window, we felt the need to impress him.

All of which is to say that I have some degree of field-trip phobia.

When my daughter announced her class was taking a field trip, I involuntarily shrieked "No!" but then had to realize that it was doubtful the kindergarten classes were going to prison or the dookie factory.

Indeed, it was the zoo. This would be safe and fun, I thought. Animals frolicking—what could go wrong?

Well, for starters, the baboon, who was frankly obsessed with amorous activities that didn't require a partner.

"What's he doing?" a few of the kids asked.

My husband, who was the only man who had come along to chaperone, decided he would deal with this question, and deal with it he did.

"That's just the traditional baboon way of waving hello," he said, sounding remarkably poised and knowledgeable.

"Oh," a little boy in the class said. "Should we wave back?"

"Oh, God no."

Next up: the "desert habitat" where an ancient camel proceeded to amuse the children by leaning down to eat his own shit. Without even moving his legs, the giraffe savored every bite as if it were the Christmas ham.

"*Oooh, icky gross!* I think I'm gonna *hurl!*"

"It's just nature," said one of the kids, trying to comfort my husband.

Not only are field trips different these days, but the very games that kids play on the playground are actually designed to prevent competition.

I know this because, at my daughter's elementary school "activity day," there wasn't a single game of Kill or Red Rover in evidence, much less Kill's kinder, gentler cousin, dodgeball.

And gone was the highly sexist game that we used to play back in the Wonder Years, the one that required all us girls to wait coyly for the arrival of a line of boys who would loudly announce, "Bum-bum-bum, here we come, all the way from Washing-*ton*." I forget most of it except that when the boys shouted "Where are you from?" (or, actually, "Where y'all fum?") we had to shout out, "Pretty Girls Station!" then squeal and run away from those baaaad boys from Washing*ton*. Perhaps they were future lobbyists.

The boys then chased the "pretty girls," and the game ended with a lot of bloody knees and general playground mayhem. No mayhem is allowed these days. Ditto "horse-play" and "roughhousing."

Kill has been banned from public school playgrounds for quite some time. Apparently the message of throwing a ball as hard as you could at an opponent who was then locked in "prison" but could get "paroled to kill again" was just a tad un-PC. Unless you were the kind of kid who longed to play on Chuckie Manson's T-ball team, Kill wasn't real appealing. After all, the game ended only when everyone on one team was "officially dead."

I was vastly relieved to see that Red Rover had also disappeared. As the smallest kid in first grade, I dreaded Red Rover and pined to sit in the shade beside my classmate Michelle, a plucky little girl who had to wear a clunky metal back-and-neck brace and read during recess, looking up only to sigh in disgust as the limbs of her classmates were snapped in the name of "fun."

In Red Rover, the biggest, burliest boy would try to break through the weakest link (Yoo-hoo! That would be *me*) of knotted-up arms and elbows. I would always just shake my arm away and let him come through, much to the horror of my teammates.

Of course, I was also the first one "called over," as in, "Red Rover, Red Rover, send the shrimpy kid over!" I would then pitifully pretend to break through the linked arms of the other team before going, "Oh! You got me. I'll just sit over here with the girl with the screws in her skull."

When I asked my daughter who won the egg-on-a-spoon race, she said she didn't know 'cause it was "just for fun."

Okay. But would it have killed 'em to keep score?

Although playground games aren't allowed to be competitive, we parents find ways to compete, such as with homework. Parents love to complain about how much homework their kids have to do every night. It's our generation's equivalent of the old walking to school, uphill both ways, in the snow, with *rickets!*

You think *your* kid has too much homework? Please, they say, waving a hand dismissively in your face: "My kid spends an average of eight-point-six hours per night just on *math*. Hell, he hasn't had a bath since 1998. There is simply no time."

To hear most parents tell it, Little Johnnie is so devoted to his homework studies that he breaks only long enough to accept a tray of soup and cold cheese sandwiches slipped through the slot in his bedroom door.

Soccer practice? Ha!

Scouts? Who's got the time?

Karate? Piano? Birthday parties? You must be kidding.

There must be too much homework. What else could explain those horrid wheeled backpacks that zip through school hallways at breakneck speeds, slicing ankles and tripping those unfortunate enough to be in their path? (If I get tripped by one more Diva Starz suitcase on wheels, I'm going to *lose it!* Oops, too late.) These backpacks the size of Guam (which, as I recall from my own geography homework days, is a small country somewhere between Chile and Mustard) must surely contain all the papers and books vital to completion of the night's homework.

These days, to hear the parents tell it, it's all homework, all the time.

Except, well, actually, it isn't.

We know this now, thanks to a study by the Brookings Institution, a famous Washington think tank. (Motto: "Well, yes, as a matter of fact, you *are* stupider than us.")

The researchers found that, in most cases, too much homework is, uh, a myth, and that truthfully, the great majority of kids have less than one hour of homework a night.

Not only that, but homework has actually decreased every year since 1984. At this rate, pretty soon your kid should be able to finish homework for five classes in a SpongeBob commercial break.

This is great news for the parents who actually do all that homework. Anybody who's ever been to a typical school science fair will quickly deduce that it's incredibly difficult for most seven-year-olds to build a scale model of the space shuttle complete with astronauts that pee real Tang.

So how did we get the idea that American kids are "over-studying"? (As I write this, a Japanese seventh-grader is laughing hysterically somewhere.) Well, some of them are, but just one in ten, and, yes, we know that's probably *your* kid and we should just shut up.

Face it. We can't credibly whine about homework anymore. I know. I'm going to miss it, too.

So what do we do if we can't compete on the playground or in homework?

We resort to Terrific Kids competitions.

To tell the truth, I was never real fond of those "I've got a terrific kid!" bumper stickers you see on the steroidal SUVs in the carpool line.

I mean, everybody's kid is terrific, right?

What kind of insecure weirdness is at work when we must have a bumper sticker on our car just so everybody else will believe it, too?

Who cares? Should we drive more carefully in the presence of a vanload of Officially Designated Terrific Kids?

("Watch 'em, Marvin; that's the future of our country ridin' in that Yukon.")

What kind of a parent believes that this "terrific kid" endorsement is an accurate tool for predicting future successes?

Yoo-hoo! Over here, everyone! That would be me.

It's not easy to admit that at the Terrific Kids assembly at my daughter's school, I was as green as a toad when two of her friends were designated "terrific" and stepped to the stage to receive their stickers and certificates.

The very, very smallest part of me wondered, "What's so terrific about them?"

They're adorable, sure. Good students, absolutely. Helpful and obedient? Check.

So where's *our* bumper sticker?

Oh, this is just so embarrassing. I've now officially become one of the people I used to make fun of. What's worse, I'm not sure it won't rub off on my kid. Will she take on my awful competitive nature and begin to say things like, "Hmmmm, sure would be a shame if something were to happen to Little Susie to make her somehow less 'terrific'!"

I don't think I have to worry about that just yet. So far, my kid seems oblivious of any of this and prefers to concentrate on her poetry studies, which are frankly limited these days to *Girls go to college to get more knowledge / boys go to Jupiter to get more stupider.*

Parents show up for the Terrific Kids assembly with

camcorders and *bouquets of flowers*. So now, the kids who don't get flowers from their parents pout, and the ones who did get flowers have won the unspoken "My parents love me better than yours love you" contest.

I swear it almost makes me long for Red Rover.

8

The One and Done Club

Sure, I Could've Thrown a Litter Like You, but How Much Ballet Can a Mom Take?

My mom-friends and I have decided that it's going to be a looooong summer now that the kids have been out of school for eighteen days, eleven hours, and twenty-six minutes. Not that we're counting.

There's one mommy in the group, okay, me, who crudely scratches lines, diagonally crossing every four, to show how many days of "summer vacation" have passed. I feel like Tom Hanks's character in *Cast Away,* only I haven't started talking to a soccer ball wearing a face drawn with my own blood. Yet.

There's a noticeable difference between my mom-friends who sagely scheduled summer camps for their kids and, uh, the rest of us.

"After book-publishing camp," one said smugly, "Sallie Jo

will do one week each of Tuscan cookery and Tae Bo, and then we'll round out July with horse camp, cursive hand-writing camp, and pre-Olympic diving."

Those of us who rejected the notion of a rigidly sched-uled summer of activities (that's right, the *crazy* ones) are cursing that we said, a mere eighteen days, eleven hours, and twenty-six minutes ago, "Children don't need all this organized activity! They need free play time!"

Well, no. That's why they call them children. They need a nice, paid instructor to show them pipe cleaner crafts and oversee relay races all day. What they apparently *don't* need, much to my shock, is a ham sandwich in front of *Days of Our Lives* with Mommy.

When my daughter complained of boredom the other day, I said, as lovingly as possible, "Shhhh! Lexie's gettin' ready to tell Abe that Brandon's the father of her love child. Don't you know nothing about a story arc?"

She sighed heavily and retreated to her room to read a book. Freak.

I guess the thing I hadn't counted on was that, even on a day like yesterday, which included a three-hour playdate with a friend, a T-ball game, and a birthday party at an amusement park, my daughter would actually say, "I'm booorred" in the twenty-three-odd minutes we had be-tween rushing from place to place.

My daughter and her friends are under the delusion that they're tiny passengers on an invisible cruise ship, and we moms are the cruise directors. ("First up, Styrofoam peanut tower construction, followed by Slip'N Slides and slushies on the Lido deck at fourteen hundred hours!")

My friend, also the mother of an only child, promised to wave to me from the back of the white van after she gets her arm out of the straitjacket that she'll surely be wearing by summer's end.

I'm sure she's exaggerating. I don't think you can really get an arm out of one of those things.

One of the only camps I did sign up for was ballet camp. I've always wanted to be one of those dedicated and cheerful "ballet moms" who researches summer dance camps for months and even sells cookie dough and Christmas wrapping paper for ballet school fund-raisers.

Ballet is beautiful, but I'm a new soul, incapable of appreciating scene after scene of young girls standing on their toes and mincing about and then standing on their toes and mincing about some more. And the plots? Sneaky fairies and magic feathers and stuff. Oh, just let me eat my own flesh till I quietly disappear. Still, the princess likes it a lot, so off we went to see her school perform something called *Coppélia*.

Now for those of you who don't know pointe from pintos, *Coppélia* is a famous comedic ballet. Like most ballets, the plot is paper thin but, hell-o, what can I say? The male lead gave me new interest in ballet. On account of he was FG. Fully gorgeous, I mean. I saw Baryshnikov perform years before he was reduced to playing one of Carrie's many boyfriends on *Sex and the City,* so I know a little about how a well-placed man in tights can give you a, uh, deeper appreciation of ballet.

Coppélia is pretty to watch, I suppose, but the plot is maddening: handsome dude falls in lust with a mannequin, thinking she's real (he's purty, but he's dumb); his fiancée finds out and gets jealous; fiancée exposes mannequin for the fake she is; handsome dude and fiancée have huge church wedding and live happily ever after.

Okay, how stupid do you have to be to go ahead and marry a man who just dumped you *for a mannequin?* But this is ballet, friends, and it's all part of the damn magic.

I don't "get" ballet. Take *Giselle,* for instance. In this one, a simple peasant girl named, well, Giselle, falls in love with a nobleman in disguise. When she finds out who he really is, and that he's betrothed to another, she has, like, a giant hissy fit and dances herself to death. Literally! Of course, because it's ballet, nothing is as it seems, and Giselle's love survives being buried. Unfortunately, she never manages to shake the Evil Queen. (Ballet is real big on Evil Queens.) She goes back to the grave, and her true love grieves for her forever and ever. This doesn't exactly put us all in the mood for pie, now, does it?

Or what about *Firebird,* another famous ballet, in which a guy named Ivan wanders into a "mysterious forest" inhabited by a magical firebird. Ivan cons the bird out of a "magic feather" that will keep him safe from the evil in the garden, including spells by mad magicians and such. I know. I'll bet you could've used a magic feather the last time you were "enchanted" by a mad magician, too, huh? Anyway, the firebird returns to help and lulls the forest monsters to sleep. In return, Ivan agrees to smash the magic egg that has cast a spell of evil over the forest forever. In the end, life gets really good in the forest, though there is no mention of cable.

All of this is fine if you're into it, but I'd much rather watch Denzel in *Man on Fire* for like the bazillionth time. That part where he puts the explosives up the bad guy's ass and then sets the timer and hands it to him? Now *that's* entertainment!

The princess loves ballet, though, so I attempt to be supportive.

Over the years, I've discovered that there are two kinds of ballet moms at our school: First, there's the kind that stays the whole hour watching anxiously through the cut-out window, enjoying every inch of little Cherish Rae's progress while monitoring the student–teacher ratio in case she needs to complain to the director. Which she will.

And then, there's the other kind, like me. We use that same hour to buy an entire week's worth of groceries, careening back into the parking lot just as class ends and the kids are getting their hands stamped with cute little red-ink ballerina figures.

When she was really little, I used to try to con my kid. "You were great!" I gushed, trying desperately to hide the eighteen bags of groceries that had magically overflowed into the backseat. Well. Her father believes there's a grocery fairy—why can't she?

There's also the carpool fairy, which would be me, if you can envision any fairy being twenty pounds overweight and wearing a shirt her kid tie-dyed over UNC sweatpants.

I've chauffered my daughter all over town this summer, not just to ballet. I have to admit that I'm going to miss, sort of, the backseat chatter that has kept me amused and confused.

You see, little girls have a ginormous capacity to giggle at things that no one over ten would ever "get." My personal least favorite is the game where one says, "I one an elevator," and the next one says, "I two an elevator," and, ohmigod, we can see where this is heading, eventually: "I eight (ate) an elevator." Hilarity ensues. They never get tired of this game, even though the "joke" is pretty obvious after the first ten or twelve items.

This summer, much of the backseat banter has concerned teen idols, or as we like to call them in our household, Chad Michael Murray.

DAUGHTER SOPHIE: Oh, Chad Michael Murray is *really* cool. A girl in my arts camp said she knows somebody whose cousin lives next door to him, and she can get his autograph for us!

FRIEND: (Brain-piercing squeal) *Eeeeeeee!* That. Is. So. Totally. Cool.

SOPHIE: That's right, and guess what?

FRIEND: What?

SOPHIE: I forget!

FRIEND: Yeah! Me, too!

(Loud, prolonged giggles for roughly eight minutes while you wonder if constant exposure to high-pitched noises can sever your brain stem. I do know for a fact that certain noises can make you nuts. A kindly woman at church once gave my daughter a "talking prayer bear" that recited the Lord's Prayer. Sadly, it was with a thick Japanese accent. You haven't really lived until you've tucked your baby into bed and heard her recite what sounds like a badly dubbed Jackie Chan movie ending with a karate-chop "Ahhh-*men!*" Back in the car, though.)

SOPHIE: I like Bratz but not Yasmin. Mommy says Yasmin looks too skanky.

FRIEND: What's skanky?

SOPHIE: It means pretty. But in a grown-up way. Like Mommy's kinda skanky, not young or anything.

FRIEND: I get it. My mommy's skanky, too!

SOPHIE *(pausing for effect)*: Well, is she stanky, too?

FRIEND: *Eeeeeeeee!* (squealing and uncontrolled spewing of McDonald's chocolate milk all over backseat of trusty Taurus)

And, while we're on the subject, memo to Morgan Spurlock, who made the fabulous and shocking documentary *Super Size Me,* in which he almost dies after eating McD's food three times a day for a month. Dude—thanks for *ruining my life*. No more fast food after watching that one. Now I have to "plan menus" and "buy groceries" and, ohmigod again, "cook."

It could be lots worse, I guess. At least I don't stank.

Chauffeuring my kid around town has gotten harder now that there's a new law requiring kids under eight to use booster car seats for safety's sake.

Have you ever tried to tell a kid who's been out of a car seat for more than a year that she must get back in one because it's the law?

ME: Honey, remember that car seat that you were so happy to get out of when you were six? The one that your eight-year-old friend used to laugh at?

SEVEN-YEAR-OLD *(warily)*: Yeeessss?

ME *(very quickly)*: Well, they changed the law, and now you're going to have to get back on that booster seat until you weigh eighty pounds, so if you don't like the idea, you better start eating a *lot* of macaroni and cheese really quick.

KID: So let me get this straight. Fat kids don't have to use a booster seat?

ME: Honey, *fat* is a very negative word. In the South, we prefer to use words and phrases such as *big-boned,* or *prosperous,* but never fat. It's quite rude."

KID: Are you serious? I have to ride in a car seat again? *Like a baby?* Why don't you just rent me some Wiggles videos and make my humiliation complete?

ME: Hon, all your friends will be in booster seats, too. Well, I mean, except for the fat ones. Oh, sorry! And look, it's not like the car seat really little kids use, the one with the vomity-smelling padded bar in front and all those dried Cheerios in the cushions. It's just the booster seat. No one will even know you're sitting on it.

KID: How long do I have to do this?

ME: Well, like I said, you have to hit eighty pounds or until you're eight years old.

KID: My life is over.

ME: Oh, honey, don't be so dramatic. It's for your own good.

KID: Can't we just say that I'm eight years old in case you get pulled over?

ME: That's lying!

KID: What about the time we went to the circus and you said I was five when I was really six so you could save five bucks on admission?

ME: Well, that's different. You were acting five that day.

KID: It's not fair. How can they change the rules?

ME: Dunno, sweetie. You got two choices. Suck it up for a few months or gain twenty-three pounds by January first.

KID: Was that a Krispy Kreme we just passed?

Getting out of the car seat is a rite of passage that's right up there with losing a tooth.

It means that your baby's growing up. I'll never forget

when my daughter, then five, held her fist out to me, then opened it slowly.

There, in the palm, was one perfect, pearly tooth that had inexplicably escaped its rightful home in her mouth.

"The Tooth Fairy's gonna come tonight!" Sophie squealed and danced around the kitchen clutching the tiny tooth while pointing to the hole where it used to be, bottom front and center.

"Swell," I said, finishing my coffee and dabbing my eyes. This was more in-your-face proof that my baby was growing up. I launched into a pathetic recitation of all the wonderful meals that little tooth had chomped on, the zillions of chicken nuggets, the pizzas, the broccoli and carrots. Yeah, okay, I made up those last two.

Then it dawned on me. Trying to be cagey, I said, "Hmmm, by the way, how much does the Tooth Fairy pay for teeth these days, do you know?"

"Well, Lucy got *seventy dollars*."

Lucy's my daughter's rich friend. Every kid should have one. Lucy's mother would never shriek, "I told you we ain't paying for that shit" if she gave away all her Lifetouch school pictures, including the "Bonus Little Patriot" flag-embossed keychain before she even got home like my kid did.

This was a Teachable Moment, though. It was time, once again, for a reminder of How Things Used to Be.

"Darling, when Mommy was a little girl, I got a shiny quarter from the Tooth Fairy, right under my pillow."

"You're kidding, right?"

"Well, back in Mommy's day, that was about half of what you'd need to buy the latest forty-five from Creedence Clearwater Revival."

"Huh?"

"CCR. You know, 'Bad Moon Rising'?"

"Were they better than Maroon Five?"

"Uh. Well, actually, no."

Later that day, I decided to poll the mommies on how much the Tooth Fairy brings.

Most said between five and ten bucks for a first tooth. I decided the tooth fairy would bring five dollars and a disclaimer that all future teeth would bring one dollar.

"What's a dis-claim-er?" my daughter asked, reading the letter the next morning.

"Well, it's like those things at the bottom of ads for prescription drugs that tell you in little print that there's a halfway decent chance that if you take the pill, it'll cure you but you'll also get excessive ear hair and a craving to eat dirt."

"Oh."

Later, I discovered there's no pleasing the mommies. One said five bucks was ridiculously high; another said she wouldn't consider giving less than twenty dollars for a First Tooth. But she's the one who dressed as the fairy and made little fairy dust footprints on her daughter's carpet so we all know she's a nut job, right?

Having an only child means that we get only one chance to do it right. There isn't going to be a do-over, and there's always some well-meaning person to point that out.

The perky hostess at the family-friendly restaurant looked at our little party of three, still wearing church clothes and thinking only of cinnamon pancakes.

"Just one child?" she asked, digging into a basket for crayons and a kiddie menu containing enough activities for a cross-country drive.

"Well, yes," said my husband, a trifle defensively. "Of course, there are days when she *seems* like more than one, but, no, it's just one. I mean we were kind of late getting started, if you know what I mean, and we're not getting any younger and so we just decided—"

"Oh, for God's sake, shut up," I hissed. "She just wants to know how many kid menus to grab."

"Oh."

As parents of an only child, we're used to the "just one child" comment. There's never any malice in it; at least I don't think there is.

Occasionally, well-meaning friends will beam and say things like, "I know *she's* not spoiled!"

Well, of course she is. And if I'd thrown a litter like some of them did, they'd all be spoiled, too. What's your point?

Very occasionally, someone will tsk-tsk and say things like "I bet you want a little brother or sister" to our daughter, and my jaw just drops.

"I'm forty-six years old!" I want to scream at them. I mean, sure, I don't look it. . . . Anyway, where am I supposed to get one of those? It's not like they're hanging out on an end cap at Target, and I don't want to be one of those freaks you read about in the *Enquirer* that had a kid with "borreyed" eggs at age eighty-six or some such.

Besides, there are plenty of folks who should have stopped at one kid. Or none. Like Michael Jackson, who, when he's not fighting child molestation charges busies himself playing with the Elephant Man's pelvis.

Frankly, I don't have the patience for more than one kid. I have plenty of mom-friends who smile dreamily and Madonna-like as their many children crawl on them, draw on the walls, and throw up on the carpet.

Still, it's surprising when strangers take it upon themselves to comment on the sad state of the only child.

"I had a friend who was an only child," the lady in line at the drugstore volunteered. "She used to spend all her time talking to her imaginary brothers and sisters, poor little thing."

Save your pity, toots. One is only the loneliest number in bad Three Dog Night songs. Believe it.

9

Toyland, Joyland

Is That a Bratz Boot in Your Sofa Cushion, or Are You Just Glad to See Me?

My daughter says that what she really wants for Christmas is an American Girl doll named Nellie. Sophie even circled the picture in the catalog and scribbled *Please!!!* in blue Magic Marker.

For those who don't know, every American Girl doll represents a specific time in our nation's history. Nellie, it turns out, is the cute-but-economically disadvantaged waif friend of rich American Girl doll Samantha. She costs $108.

Some waif.

The American Girl catalog is beautifully photographed. Heck, by the time I finished looking at it, I could barely stifle an urge to order Kit, Molly, and especially the plucky Josefina complete with her authentic reproduction New Mexico sleigh bed.

Thank heavens I was reminded by the big, bold letters of the catalog's very first page: "True friendship is the greatest gift."

Indeed it is, and that's why my little girl is going to become good friends with the Nellie look-alike I found on sale for twelve bucks last week and slyly named K-Martha.

K-Martha is absolutely gorgeous and, although she doesn't come with her own line of books, bedding, and matching human-size clothing, I think she's going to be a hit.

Although they're undeniably beautiful, AGs are way too fancy and expensive to play with, so you put them up on a shelf or in a glass case and admire them. K-Martha, on the other hand, you can drag by the feet and use for the cat's pillow and it's no big deal.

Each American Girl doll comes with her own bio. Kit, who represents 1934 in our nation's history, "went from rich to poor overnight but still has spunk!" says the catalog. Oh, those wacky poor kids; at least they make us laugh!

Samantha, the most famous AG, is "a generous girl with a curious nature living in 1904." She's the one who just starred in her own TV special, so I imagine the other dolls have taken to hissing and sniping and calling her Miss Thang behind her back.

Molly represents 1944 and, for ninety-eight dollars plus shipping, comes with a "pretend steel penny." Oh, you shouldn't have.

If you get tired of watching them look historic, you can

take the Girls for a pretend ride on the official American Girl horse. He costs sixty dollars, but he looks just like a horse from the Family Dollar Store to me.

There is only one lonely American Girl boy-doll, and he's no Ken, let me tell you. Even on the catalog pages, Bitty Boy Twin looks as if he wants to scream.

I wonder why. Perhaps it's because he's sick of being dressed by chubby little hands that don't take proper care of his Fall Frolic outfit or his Festive Plaid knickers. Or maybe it's because he just read his "biography" and realizes that the high point of his life is going to be having "not-so-clean fun making cookies" with his twin sister. Hey! Who needs PlayStation?

Truthfully, I suspect Bitty Boy looks so horrified because he just read his own shipping charges or maybe he learned that all his siblings are on back order. Again.

What could possibly be more American?

How about the Easy-Bake Oven, which Sophie has begged for this year, no surprise to any mother of a little girl. But when I actually went out to buy one, I felt that awful mix of panic and disappointment I'd felt earlier in the day when I discovered they'd taken beets off the Pizza Hut salad bar. *Is nothing sacred?*

The new Easy-Bake Oven looks nothing like the one I remember as a tot. It's a microwavey "snack center" contraption. At least it still operates on a 100-watt bulb that every parent forgets to buy. It's a parental rite of passage to spend most of Christmas Day trying to figure out which bulb in the house can be unscrewed and substituted so you can watch a single "brownie" cook in just under eight hours.

The hot toys this year talk a lot more than the ones in the past, and I'm not sure this is a good thing. Diva Starz dolls, we're told, "speak fashion-related phrases!"

What the hell is a fashion-related phrase? Oh, I get it. Stuff that supermodels say. Stuff like, "I'd like a single leaf of arugula on a Wheat Thin, please, and then I'll go throw it up" or "I'd like to act, but I have no talent!"

There's also the Lil Chefs Talking "Smart" Kitchen, a seventy-dollar plastic kitchen programmed with fifty sounds and phrases "typically heard in the kitchen." I'm hoping that includes the mantras from my kitchen: "Let's just throw out this slop and go to Wendy's" or "Don't answer that; it's a telemarketer!"

Maybe your kid aspires to be a fry cook. The McDonald's Food Cart comes with a little headset just like the drive-through guy wears, presumably so you can pretend to mutter unintelligible gibberish to whoever you're playing with and they can scream, "What? What did you say?" just like the real drive-through.

There's even a talking Lemonade Lisa who dispenses lemonade-type product to a pretend customer while uttering "10 fun phrases!" Personally I'd prefer a mini-Starbucks stand where pretend customers would complain nonstop about spending nearly five bucks for a large latte.

I may settle for a Fisher-Price Sweet Magic Kitchen, which has pretend food that turns colors to let you know it's done. Ohhhhh. So that's how you can tell.

Of course, the best toys at this stage always seem to involve Barbie & Co. My daughter's little friend gave her a pregnant Midge doll for her birthday this year. It was a regular stroll down memory lane, I tell you. When I was a kid, I had Barbie and my sister had Midge, a perky, freckle-faced redhead with a Dutchboy hairdo. She was the girl next door, the pretty-in-pink-plaid pal, the also-ran to her hottie friend, the Barbster.

I always felt a bit smug that I had Barbie while sis had Midge. You just knew things were going to be harder for Midge. And now she's knocked up.

The funniest thing is the brouhaha from the freaks that are offended by this sort of thing. Turns out some Wal-Mart stores, exposing retail spines of Jell-O, have taken to hiding the massive Midge behind the counter during the Christmas season so shoppers wouldn't be "offended" by the bun in the oven.

Wonder what they do with those pictures of Mary riding the donkey into Bethlehem and great with child. Is that okay, you think?

Frankly, we love pregnant Midge. The baby's daddy, says a rather defensive Mattel, is her longtime husband, Alan, who has been chronically inferior over the years to the buff Ken.

While Barbie and, to a much lesser degree, Ken have been carving out careers in everything from aerospace engineering to professional surfing, Midge and Alan have just been getting by, shopping the sales and buying extras for their tacky-but-clean singlewide with S & H Greenpoints. And now, the blessed event!

Turns out Baby Doctor Barbie (yes, there is one) is rumored to have delivered Midge's baby, at least so says Mattel in a press release. Oh, it just always has to be about Barbie, doesn't it? You just know she patted Midge's swollen fingers and said condescending things about how she'd get her shape back just like she did. Why, Midge, says Barbie, you'll be back to winning Olympic gold medals in no time, just like me.

Of course, she's Midge, so we know that she's Everywoman, operating on real-world rules that mean her butt will remain as lumpy as undercooked grits for the rest of her polystyrene life.

The pregnant Midge doll, much to Sophie's delight, actually delivers the baby sans soap-opera squealing scenes and similar unpleasantness. No "Push! Push!" words of encouragement from Alan, just lift up the rounded belly flap, and out drops the curled-up infant! What could be more fabulous? (Having had a C-section, I can relate to Midge. I should warn her that, for the next three days, nosy Dr. Barbie will be in her face demanding to know if she's "passed gas yet" while Alan uses this as a chance to invite the nurse to pull his finger, so very Alan.)

I have to wonder what Midge and Alan must make of Barbie's recent, uh, dalliance.

It was *très* shocking when we learned recently that Barbie had actually given Ken the old "I need some space" speech and taken up with Blaine, a "hunky Australian surfer dude" several years her junior.

At the time, those of us who have applauded Barbie's enviable ability to morph from movie star to pet doctor to airline pilot were worried about her mental stability.

After all, Ken, whose only downside was waxy buildup on his hair, was always supportive of Barbie's myriad career changes. Only adult ADHD, or perhaps a movie-star acceptable level of manic depression, could explain this compulsion to try so many different careers. No matter what she undertook, Ken was always there, in his cardigan and khakis or swim trunks or dinner jacket, championing his beloved's latest lark.

Blaine, on the other hand, just doesn't seem that reliable. He's the type who would cheat on Barbie with one of those Bratz sluts and then lie about it in the morning, even as Barbie discovered the creepy telltale amputeed boot in Blaine's sofa cushions.

Barbie didn't pick a great time to start thinking outside the (cardboard) box. Blaine, it turns out, isn't selling all that well. The only question left is, now that third-quarter earnings are down 26 percent, will Barbie reconcile with Ken?

Ken, if you're reading this, don't take the ho back. You're too good for her. Don't let the suits at Mattel try to put you back by Barbie's side. She dumped you after forty-three years for a tanned boy toy in board shorts, and you're gonna come crawling back?

Dude.

Those of us who have looked up to Barbie for her career achievements recognized Ken as the wind beneath her wings. And not just professionally. Ken would be the one who would lovingly wipe the rice pudding from Barbie's perfect chin when the two of them eventually relocated to adjoining rooms at Mattel's assisted living complex. Blaine? He's too busy chasing other Sheilas, pounding Foster's lager, and hanging out with his surf buddies, all of whom look depressingly like Ashton Kutcher.

Barbie's new beau is, from sales figures and appearances, simply not working out.

So, what to do? First, hire a publicist to handle the inevitable media hordes that will want to know where their love went. An immediate "they will remain good friends" press release must be distributed.

Ken and Alan should start hitting the bars together. Alan, as we all know, probably has a tab at every watering hole in Mattelville. Maybe with Ken in the mix, he'll actually be allowed back inside one or two of them.

Expect Ken to play hard to get for a while, but I predict he'll be back. After four decades, he's proved to be a capable lapdog. I only hope that he reminds Barbie every now and again that he could've had Midge any time he wanted.

But then, again, who couldn't?

10

Slacker Moms Unite!

Say *Adios!* to All That Guilt

Everywhere I turn lately, there's a magazine cover, newspaper headline, or book jacket screeching about how the modern mom is trying to do it all and failing miserably.

Shuttling her kids from soccer to fencing to swim class to flute lessons, today's Supermom is frazzled, resentful, and depressed. In interview after interview, she wonders why motherhood isn't the fun gig she imagined.

Maybe because I came to motherhood a bit later in life than most, I've never really tried to overachieve and now, at last, my slackness has been rewarded.

Slacker moms are in!

Pulitzer Prize–winning columnist Anna Quindlen wrote glowingly about her own slacker mom recently. The woman couldn't even drive, and she usually answered, "I dunno, he's around here somewhere" when one of Anna's brothers went missing, but "wherever she was, was home."

She didn't worry about her kids not getting accepted in the town's best gymnastics class; she just told them to get out from under her and play outside. Radical!

Ever since I gave birth, I've watched with a mix of horror and admiration those mommies who do it all. They work full-time, lead Scout troops, and volunteer to host foreign exchange students. They exercise for an hour every day, shuttle their kids all over town, cook nutritious meals, and collapse every night for five hours of tortured sleep.

Finally, they've gone from a low hum of discontent to a full-fledged whine. And all I can say is this: It's About Damn Time.

It turns out that "slacker moms" like me are considered to be the ones who are truly mentally healthy. I know—scary isn't it?

The mantra of the slacker mom should always be: "Do just enough to get by." Try saying it, supermoms. It's really quite exhilarating.

Here's how we do it.

ANNOYING WELL-INTENTIONED PERSON: Hi, Celia! I was just wondering if you'd be willing to organize (host, train, serve as, volunteer, mentor, etc.) so-and-so?

ME: No.

See how easy?

At first you'll no doubt feel guilty, but stand firm. Your sanity is at stake. Put your feet up; watch *Oprah*. Let your kid play. Do Just Enough to Get By.

I'm sure that a few of you diehards are saying, "Well, that's fine for you, but that leaves us to do all the work!"

I know! Isn't it fabulous? Look, martyrdom's overrated. If you resent it, stop the hell doing it.

Here at Slacker Mom Central, I will continue to do just enough to get by on the extracurricular front.

Okay, to be honest, as soon as my one term as Spanish coach is over.

See even we hardcore slacker moms can get sucked in occasionally.

After telling everyone that slacking off and refusing to volunteer for anything is fabulously freeing, I heard myself say, in a small voice, yes, when I was recruited to help with the after-school Spanish club.

I don't even know how it happened, so just let this be a lesson to all of you aspiring slackers. Perhaps an exact transcript of the conversation can help us figure out what went wrong.

NICE MOM: Celia, will you help with the new Spanish Club after school? I know your daughter's signed up, and we desperately need volunteers.

ME *(snorting)*: You must be desperate, toots. The only Spanish I know is Nachos Bell Grande and Jose Cuervo.

(See, so far, so good. I'm standing firm. So why am I

now riding around with a backseat full of piñata-making materials?)

NICE MOM *(cheerily)*: Oh, that's okay! You don't have to speak Spanish to help out.

(Now here's where I should have sniffed el rat-o. She's killing me with kindness, and I'm falling for it. See what happens next.)

ME: You don't? (I thought this was strange. Does this mean that I can finally perform surgery without having to attend that pesky medical school?)

NICE MOM: Heck no! (Okay, here's a bad sign; never trust cheery women who say Midwesterny-sounding things like "heck!" There's just something not right about them.)

NM: Really, we just need people to help pass out materials and maybe keep the kids from getting too loud.

ME: Uh, okay, I guess.

I have no idea what hit me. Was it because she was so relentlessly cheerful? Was it the thought of being able to jerk a knot in somebody else's kid for a change?

The next day, I reported for duty at the school cafeteria, where one of the mom-leaders came over and asked if I'd mind reading a book or two in Spanish to the kids.

I'd been hoo-doo'ed by the chipper Midwesterner. Of course they expected me to speak Spanish.

"No hablo español," I said weakly.

"Oh, good! You're fluent!"

Another corralled volunteer looked at me helplessly. "I've had six years of French," she said.

"No problemo," I assured her. "It's probably a lot the same. Just substitute a lot of choppy sounds for that jeh-jeh-jeh-joosh stuff the French say. Oh! And be sure to add an *o* to the end of everything. I seem to remember that from high school."

"Okay-o," she said gamely.

Once the kids learned to count to twenty in Spanish, it was time to play Spanish Bingo, which is a lot like English Bingo except with a lot less cigarette smoke and black hair dye.

I looked at my watch and realized that we'd been at it for about twelve minutos. What on earth were we going to do for the rest of the hour?

Thank goodness, our fearless leader ("I had to learn Spanish cuz I married me a Mexican") was on the case. Everyone would learn how to say his or her name in *español*.

This reminded me of Spanish 1 class when we did the same thing. While I had fantasized that my Spanish name would be exotico, it turned out to be exactly the same as it was in English.

"But I want to be Rosalita or something," I had whined to the beleaguered teacher.

"Oh, yeah?" she asked. "Well, I wanna be Doris Day, but that ain't happening either."

Muy harsh.

So, I've lost some of my slacker mom street cred, but not all of it. A few days after Spanish Club ended for the year, a coven of Supermoms approached me about helping with a new Brownie troop.

"No @##$ way," I said, feeling the smug surge of power that comes from being such a committed slack-ass. The only Brownies I had any interest in, I told them, came out of a Duncan Hines box.

They skittered away to hassle some other victim, no doubt hissing the whole time about my "lack of commitment" and my "refusal to be a team player" and my "really wide brownie-eating ass."

Those Supermoms can be real bitches when you think about it.

We could all take a lesson from men, if you ask me. Because no matter how slack a dad is, if he does the least little thing, people gush over him.

When I went on a business trip a while back, everyone marveled at the "good job" my husband did.

Why is that? Is it like seeing a chimpanzee play the clarinet? Sure, it's possible, but you don't honestly expect to ever see it in your lifetime.

Or is it like the Arkansas rooster I remember from childhood? The one that could take your dollar bill, punch a cash register, and give you change back? He even had his own *postcard*. Is someone, somewhere, printing a postcard with a similar apparent freak of nature? The caring daddy who managed to not completely screw up a week of single parenthood?

"Your husband did *such* a good job," cooed a teacher at our daughter's elementary school.

"You should have seen how, when he realized it was PE day, he just flew out the door and went home so he could get her tennis shoes!" gushed another. "She's one lucky little girl!"

A woman whom I don't even know stopped to tell me that my husband "sure was a great dad while you were gone!"

What was next? A memo from the central office announcing that the school's name would be changed to honor him?

Again, I ask, Why is it a man performs the minimal task of getting his kid to and from school dressed in anything that's not Hello Kitty pajamas and he's all of a sudden frickin' Keanu dismantling a bomb on a city bus?

Feeling ridiculously guilty, I renounced my slacker mom status temporarily and immediately signed up to take pecan tartlets to the teachers' tea. Where was my ticker tape parade? Who judged the schoolwide essay contest every year? Who had been class mom for three years in a row? (Okay, y'all know it wasn't me but it *could* have been.)

Clearly, after a week away, my stock was low. Plus, I'd gotten into a fight with the carpool Nazis that morning.

"We just want it safe for the children," one hissed at me.

Because I was holding my daughter's hand and we were *on foot,* I failed to see a threat here. What were we in danger of doing? Taking out a few roly-polys before their time?

"You shouldn't walk here! You should walk there!" the second carpool Nazi screeched, sounding rather like a hostile Dr. Seuss and pointing to a space approximately two feet away.

Jesus. Give somebody a Day-Glo vest and they think they rule the world.

That night, I told my husband that his favorite slacker-mom had once again gotten it wrong. I'd offended the carpool volunteers.

"You didn't?" he fairly shrieked.

"Yeah, so what?"

"I have to *live* with these people," he moaned.

"Not anymore. Slacker mom's back on the job now, remember?"

"Oh, yeah," he said, brightening. "What's for supper?"

PART II

Celebrities

11

Celebrity Moms

Don't Hate Them Because They're Beautiful
(When There Are So Many Other Reasons to Hate Them!)

I'm sure that y'all are just as relieved as I am that actress Denise Richards had her baby and it weighed, like, five pounds or some similar celebrity-baby weight.

Our long national nightmare is over. Denise was starting to rival Kate Hudson for the longest gestation. Celebrities announce their pregnancies through their publicists on the morning after conception and thus begins the very long season of photos in the park of them wearing ball caps, their two-hundred-dollar tank tops stretched tight over blossoming tummies.

Celebrities generally don't give birth to big, fat, standard American babies. They tend to work out during their pregnancies, drinking wheat grass shakes and nibbling on sun-dried particleboard. Then, immediately after the birth, they hire a full-time personal trainer to whip them back into their prepregnancy weight of roughly ninety-four pounds.

If there was any way they could insert a tiny home gym into the womb and encourage the baby to start working out *now,* they would. ("Hush now, little Artemis. No pain, no gain!")

Celebrities are not like you and me, my hons. And not just because they eat with their feet. No, no, it's because they don't even call babies what they are. They call them *bumps.* An entire cover story in *People* magazine was devoted to showcasing the bumps of Gwyneth Paltrow, Carnie ("Would somebody please tell me again why the hell I had gastric bypass surgery?") Wilson, and "double bumpers" Marcia Gay Harden and Julia Roberts.

Celebrities also tend to wear skin-tight clothing through-out pregnancy, a look that is, as I have said before, just plain wrong. Yes, we get it, you're pregnant and you're fabu-lous! But we find it hard to relate. Instead of waddling into the IHOP twice a week to order "lemon crepes and keep 'em comin'" like those of us out here in the Real World, they are instead stepping up the yogilates sessions with Si-mone and Rafiki. Makes me want to snap their twiglike celebrity necks like a Cheeto.

Mmmm, Cheetos. Sorry. Where was I?

Oh, yes. Britney Spears. See, here's the thing about that celebrity mama. Britney is, at heart, just a good ol' Southern girl. I'm sure that her rich friends were horrified by her wearing that shirt that said BABY with an arrow, but I thought she was just being fashionably retro. Either that or she wanted to make sure nobody thought it was just some rogue goiter.

God bless Britney for naming her baby Sean Preston, a nice, normal name that sounds like it came straight off *The Young and the Restless,* which is where decent regular folks get their baby names. We don't name our kids things like Coco or Mosaic or some such, because we know they'd get their ass kicked on the playground. At church.

I also loved Brit for gaining, like, a gazillion pounds while pregnant. Girlfriend ate fried okra and spoonbread and mac and cheese the whole time, and I know that the other L.A. moms must've been horrified.

(Note to Britney: If Kevin starts saying you need "to drop some elbees," remind him that you could lose 140 pounds right quick with the right divorce lawyer. Hell, you've done it before. And I don't want to say Kevin Federline isn't smart. I mean, just because he believes that Geena Davis is really the president doesn't mean he's dumb, does it?)

Britney had a C-section, which is terribly un-celebritylike.

You know, it's the celebrity moms-to-be who first popularized the doula movement. Doulas are like uppity midwives; they hate drugs and forceps and anything else truly useful. They are *très* chic! I'm sure that I will now get very earnest mail from doulas and their, uh, doulettes, about how I don't understand the incredible level of support they bring to the birth process. Then again, who cares?

I suppose if I sound bitter, it is because I've seen too many photos of Denise with her baby moments after delivery, not a hair out of place, luminescent skin and tastefully understated eye makeup. You want to see what a real woman looks like moments after birth? Watch *A Baby Story* on The Learning Channel: sweat-soaked, bloodshot eyes, doula-less.

And knowing that bump isn't going any-damned-where for at least a year.

Once baby arrives, celebrities have a new dilemma. What to do with them while mom's on the set or in the recording studio.

Well, thank goodness for a new whiz-bang video program created just for the celebrity who must be away for many hours at a time. The system allows the celebrity babies to watch a computer screen that plays a slide show of the many faces of the famous mom, accompanied by a caption identifying her as MOMMY.

Hollywood moms are crazy about this because it's tiresome to constantly have to say, "No, no, little Zeitgeist, that's not Mommy; that's Nanny. Mommy just got paid many millions of dollars to simulate the devil's aerobics with Brad Pitt. Isn't Mommy a-ma-zing?"

Of course, to a six-week-old, the caption on the video might as well say *potato* or *egomaniac,* but let's not quibble here. The intention is to make sure that there is no confusion about just who the mommy is.

This way, the procession of starched and background-checked nannies will never be mistaken for the actual birth mother. I should think it might also be helpful to switch the video to have a picture of the nanny with the words NOT THE MOMMY or ILLEGAL ALIEN as caption.

Speaking of aliens, as I write this, Tom Cruise and Katie "I'm With Crazy" Holmes are expecting a celebrity pod-baby. Yes! The seed has been successfully planted and now is growing and flourishing in the formerly Catholic womb of Ms. Katie.

I say "formerly Catholic" because, as we all know, Tom Cruise is a huge Scientologist, and he likes his women like his coffee, hot and full of beans just like him.

Let's not sugarcoat this one, hons. I don't think Tom is the baby daddy. I'm not convinced that he, uh, has it in him, so to speak. My friend Courtney agrees and repeatedly refers to the Cruise kid as "that fake-ass baby." Well, I didn't say she was my nice friend.

Tom and Katie are planning a Scientology-approved method of birthing, which consists of "silent contemplation and no drugs."

Funny thing, I don't remember childbirth as a time of silent contemplation so much as a time to turn my head all the way around in a perfect 360 spin. Hey, you say *to-mah-to*.

Celebrities love Scientology, apparently because they

don't have any decent Baptist churches out in Hollywood, so they must cling to the teachings of some guy named Ron. Scientologists believe in mind over matter. One of its biggest fans is actress Kirstie Alley. So am I the only one who thinks it's funny that she finds the gospel according to Jenny Craig much more useful than that of L. Ron Hubbard in shedding all those mind-over-matter pounds?

John Travolta (maybe *he's* the baby daddy) is a huge Scientologist and his wife, Kelly Preston, is always yammering about her Scientology birthing style.

Scientologists believe that words spoken during birth are recorded in a baby's subconscious mind and can cause irrational emotions later in life.

Ooops. Do you think the phrase, "You did this to me, you scum-sucking sack of shit" screamed repeatedly over the course of nine hours counts? If so, my bad.

I think it's hilarious that the only damn time Hollywood celebrities don't do drugs is when they're giving birth. What's wrong with this picture?

Tom Cruise says that you don't need drugs to birth a baby, because drugs are the evil spawn of the pharmaceutical industry's marriage to mainstream medicine.

He is so adamant about this that he even blames psychiatry—in a crazy-man-screaming-on-the-subway kind of way—for the Holocaust. Yes, that Holocaust.

The whole *Rosemary's Baby* feel of this particular celeb coupling is just indescribably delicious. And the tabloids have a new staple: Tom dipping Katie, apparently in a rather awkward height-compensation gesture. I'm guessing poor Katie can't even walk across the kitchen for a bowl of corn-flakes without Tom springing out and dipping her.

He dips her at the supermarket, the soccer game, walking the dogs, everywhere. At last we have a replacement for the stock photo of Angelina Jolie with that eighty-pound Maddox glued to her hip or Paris Hilton with seventy-five-pound Nicole Richie glued to hers.

Oh, and speaking of Paris, she has said that she is ready to have a child. I guess this means that the future is in good hands. Of course, we don't know where they've been.

Why does Paris want kids?

"I know that kids complete your life," she said in an interview with *People* magazine. "I think having kids will make me happier than I am. Plus, I already treat my three puppies like kids!"

Yes, well, as long as you have a realistic notion of motherhood. The goal of any baby should be to bring happiness to his shallow-as-a-pie-pan mother. And if you can train that baby to eat on all fours from a five-hundred-dollar bowl bought at a Rodeo Drive boutique and shaped like a giant bone, well, so much the better!

Holy God, where is Dr. Phil when you need him? He needs to have one of those knee-touching sessions with Paris, look straight into her soulless eyes and say, "Paris, if you think raising up young'uns is the same as hauling around that

Gucci dog carrier of yours with a two-pound mutt that looks like a toilet brush with eyes, you're crazier 'n cactus juice."

Paris Hilton having a baby is just a bad idea. Parenthood is about sacrifice, and I don't mean having to choose between the dead sea mud treatment and the high colonic at your private spa.

Oh, and one more thing. If Paris is really serious about her desire to have a baby, she should probably know that if she thought that Brazilian wax was painful, she might want to hire a surrogate for the actual birthing. They're *hot*.

12

Something Stinks

And I'm Pretty Sure It's Tonya Harding

This Christmas, it seemed to me that every celebrity introduced a "signature fragrance." If all you want for Christmas is to smell just like Donald Trump, you're in luck. I haven't seen it yet, but I'm guessing that Trump Cologne smells like money. At sixty bucks for less than an ounce, it should be called Sucka. I'm sure *Apprentice* fans would love a gift set featuring Trump flanked by (much) smaller vials of George, which smells vaguely like crotchety old man, and Carolyn, which comes with its very own stick to insert up your ass, never to be removed.

Also just in time for holiday gift-giving: Britney Spears's flirty floral, Curious, rumored to attract scruffy, ill-dressed man-boys whose skills are limited to fathering children out of wedlock and—oh, sorry, that was all.

Also new this season, a citrusy mix from the folks at Adidas. Right. I'm going to buy perfume made by a company known for products that combine rubber and sweaty feet. Pass.

Paris Hilton (insert your favorite joke here) was supposed to introduce her new signature scent for the masses later, but her handlers felt that she's so hot right now that there was no sense in waiting. No name yet, but I'm rather fond of Mattressback!

Jessica Simpson has a huge line of smell'um, including a "threesome of deliciously kissable Taste." Gawd, it must be true what they always said about preachers' daughters.

Kim Cattrall, who's not really a ho but just played one on TV, has introduced Spark Seduction, and Boston Rob Mariano, a second-place finisher in TV's *Survivor,* has unveiled Foreman, which "combines scents of juniper and clean sweat." Mariano said he chose the name because he used to be a construction foreman before becoming Mr. Am-buh. Cool. I used to work in a restaurant; meet my new scent, Fry Cook.

Perhaps the weirdest celeb scent I've encountered is Full Throttle, from father-son team Paul Teutul Sr. and Jr., of *Orange County Choppers,* a cult hit on The Discovery Channel. Both Teutuls look kinda scary but, as we're reminded every year at Christmas until we just wanna puke, hardcore bikers are all just gentle giants wanting to deliver gifts to poor kids. Whatever.

The entire cast of *All My Children* has teamed with Wal-Mart to introduce Enchantment. I presume that with just one spritz you'll be transported to a fictional town where women wake up with flawless hair and makeup in the arms of their husband's best friends.

That doesn't smell; it reeks.

Of course, those are all real products available in real stores. But I believe there are so many more celebrities who could be tapped for perfume pitches. How's about Rehab, a clean new scent from Whitney Houston? (Free gift-with-purchase: Bobby Brown's spicy scent, Jail Thyme.)

Skater-turned-professional-wrestler Tonya Harding loves to talk tough, so I'm thinking her perfume might be called Smells Like Ass.

Okay, that could hurt sales.

Although the endless celebrity perfume is tiresome, it's still not so irksome as the celebrities thinking that just because they had a cameo on *Baywatch* one time, they're now ready to write for kids.

Madonna's leading the pack with an entire series of children's books. Whose idea was it to give Madonna a five-book kids' book deal? What next? A parenting book by Michael Jackson? (*What to Expect When One of Us Is Painfully Weird at Best or a Child Molester at Worst?*)

Why does every celebrity think they should write a children's book? Usually they're still feeling the last bliss of the epidural when they bark at the nurse, "Call my agent! The world *needs* my children's book!"

Sometimes it works. Fergie transformed her tattered toe-sucking image by writing a sweet series of children's books about a talking helicopter. I'm less optimistic about new poppa-of-three Jerry Seinfeld's foray into kid lit. I mean what's that gonna read like? I'm guessing: "What's the deal with porridge? I mean, is it oatmeal or is it Cream of Wheat?"

But Madonna? Does the world really need her take on Puss 'n Boots? (Then again, the original features a velvet-vested cat wearing nothing more than the vest, a smile, and some fetching thigh-high leather boots, so perhaps we have nothing to fear.)

Still, this is the woman who created a coffee table book that was so scorching, it was shrink-wrapped before it hit the stores.

One wonders what Dr. Seuss would think of Madonna's literary pursuits if he were still alive.

Perhaps something like this . . .

I would not, could not read this book
Not on a plane or by a brook
Not in a boat or on a float
So I ask you, Thing One and Thing Two
What would you, should you, have me do?
Read it? No! You ask too much!

I don't like bondage, sex, and such
What? It's sweet, it's good kids' stuff?
It's nothing nasty or even rough?
Okay, then, I shall give it a try
But keep the smelling salts standing by

Am I being harsh? Maybe. But would you let Madonna babysit your toddler? ("I spy with my little eye . . . a transvestite nun and a dozen choristers wearing nipple rings!")

I thought not.

Of course, celebrities aren't just spending their idle hours developing dubious perfumes and writing children's books. They have so much to give us all.

For instance, convicted felon and rap diva Lil' Kim has introduced a line of luxury watches that cost up to $3,500. I suppose marking time is weighing heavily on her mind these days, bless her tiny little heart.

Scruffy country crooner Willie Nelson sells BioWillie, an ecologically correct fuel that I'm guessing is composed entirely of old whiskers and sleep boogers.

You can even get a MasterCard debit card with Usher's face on it or, for the old-school types, Elvis, who continues to make huge amounts of money from the grave.

If you're having a party, don't forget the Erik Estrada gourmet chips. Did you say "Erik who?" Tsk-tsk. How could you forget his dramatic stylings as a motorcycle cop in *CHiPs*? Get it now? The chips have the bitter aftertaste of fleeting fame and broken dreams. Or maybe that was just the potassium gum.

Serve those chips with a side of Cheech Marin's Gnarly Garlic Hot Sauce. Cheech, of Cheech and Chong fame, used to be hilarious when they riffed on pot, but now he plays the gardener on *Judging Amy*. The judge better take a closer look at the plants in her mama's yard, I say.

And, finally, there's the rubber-bracelet craze ignited by Lance "Bubba" Armstrong. His Live Strong yellow rubber bracelets have raised millions for cancer research, and good for him. But don't you think we've all gotten a little carried away with the whole rubber-bracelet thing?

The other day I saw one that read ADOPT A SNIPER: ONE SHOT, ONE KILL, NO REMORSE, I DECIDE.

Kinda makes you feel all warm and gooshy inside, doesn't it.

Admittedly the sniper bands aren't nearly so popular as the ones that say DREAM and BELIEVE and even I ♥ KITTENS but it's out there.

There's even one that says NO BULLYING. I have this awful mental picture of a bespectacled, wedgie-prone, undersize middle-schooler showing that one off like Wonder Woman to the creepy bully who inevitably will steal his iPod. "But wait!" he will moan, crumpling to the floor. "Didn't you see my bracelet?"

What would Lance Armstrong think of the bracelets

that say simply BEER and SLACKER or the steel-gray one that says FBI?

Here's a hint, J. Edgar Doofus: It's unlikely that a real FBI agent would wear a rubber bracelet identifying himself that way. It would be like that fuzzy-haired undercover agent at the high school showing up in the lunchroom with a nifty tie-dye version that says NARC.

The rubber bracelets can cause confusion. If you see one embossed with a rainbow, does this mean that the wearer is gay or simply a lover of bright colors and, God forbid, unicorns?

Somewhere Lance Armstrong must be sitting in a restaurant and wondering why the teenage waitress is wearing bracelets that say HIGH MAINTENANCE, SPOILED, and DRAMA QUEEN.

And, as she turns to walk away, the faint musk of Tonya Harding trails behind her.

13

Montel's Smoking Weed

(But Will He Share with Sylvia the Psychic?)

I just read where TV talk show host Montel Williams has come out in support of legalizing marijuana for medical use. Turns out that Montel has been smoking dope for years to ease his MS symptoms. While I am happy that he has found pain relief, I have to admit that this certainly explains a lot. Everybody knows Montel's show is just one redneck family paternity test after another, with only the occasional relief of dwarf wrestling or chats with that creepy psychic lady, Sylvia something. Now we know why: The brother was high!

This should lay to rest any notion that marijuana actually makes one think more creatively. I'm picturing Montel firing up a big ol' doobie at the morning staff meeting and saying,

"A'ight, dawgs, let's do a show where we test some guy's DNA to see if he's really the father!"

While his yes-men staffers nod and say, "Great idea!" you know they're all thinking, *Tel needs to stop smokin' the chronic and give the people what they want: More Midget Weddings!*

Most of Montel's most popular shows involve repeat visits by psychic mediums. I'll admit Miss Sylvia is better than most because she just comes right out with stuff. ("Yes, your brother's in heaven and he's also sitting beside you right now. Next!") To hear Miss Sylvia tell it, we're surrounded by dead relatives, which always makes me nervous when I think about getting undressed.

Some of the TV mediums sound as if they've been getting high with Tel, though.

MEDIUM: I'm getting a message from someone named Harry. Your late father?

AUDIENCE JOE: Nope, no Harrys.

MEDIUM: Oh, my bad! Did I say Harry? I meant John.

JOE: No Johns either—sorry.

MEDIUM: He's telling me he is a pianist, this John.

JOE: Nope. But I do have a dead aunt named Clarissa who played cards a lot.

MEDIUM: Clarissa! That's who I meant, of course! (Audience cheers wildly.)

Talking about Montel getting high, wouldn't you hate to be the one in charge of bringing the little chocolate doughnuts to the morning meeting? Talk about your never-ending jobs. ("Dang I'm hawn-gry!")

Learning that Montel has basically been high since 1999 is kinda funny when you consider all those "scared straight" lectures and teen boot camps he sponsors. All he wants to do, turns out, is puff some cheeb legal-like.

And so do Walter Cronkite and Hugh Downs. That's right! I found their names, along with Montel's, on a list of celebrities who support legalizing marijuana for sick folks. And did I mention that my bunions have been driving me kuh-razy?

Says the grandfatherly Cronkite, "At the end of the day, me and the missus like to burn a coupla buddha-sticks and stare at the sunset. Dude." Okay, not really, but a girl can dream.

And Hugh "Ganja-man" Downs? Who knew? Of course, there were some nonsurprises on the list, namely Susan Sarandon and Tim Robbins, who define Hollywood hipness with their hybrid cars and illegitimate children, and Woody Harrelson, who—hello!—wears only clothes made out of hemp.

In an interview, Montel said that there are days when he doesn't even want to get out of bed.

I feel ya. The irony is that when the rich and powerful get sick, politics can get pretty strange. Witness the militaristic Montel and the conservative Nancy Reagan bravely fighting her own kind for stem-cell research. When illness hits home, it's amazing how marijuana becomes less reefer madness and more "compassionate access." Either way, I'm glad Montel's feeling groovy. Sick people should be able to find relief where they can. Word.

14

Reality Bites

Super Skanks Lewinsky and Hilton Are Fun to Watch, but Those 100-Pound Toddlers Rule!

When I first read about Fox's new reality series *The Simple Life,* I knew I wouldn't be able to resist the show about two vapid Beverly Hills honeys dumped on a rural Arkansas pig farm. I tried to fight it, hons, but, before I knew it, it was back to the Barcalounger with a box of Smart Ones éclairs, clicker in hand.

I can't resist reality TV, although I do have some standards. How's about a tiny little shout out for my refusal to watch *The Littlest Groom?*

To say that the stars of *The Simple Life,* famous ick girls Paris Hilton and Nicole Richie, appear to be shallow and self-absorbed is like saying that Joan Rivers appears to have had some cosmetic surgery.

Paris and Nicole (dumb and dumber) haven't got enough

meat on their bones to make a poor man a pot of soup, but that's not why I love to hate them. Although it certainly helps.

Of course, it doesn't take a genius to figure out why we like these Dumb Rich People shows that are sprouting up faster 'n toadstools after an Arkansas thunder-buster. They're fun to watch because we get to do a little superior dance.

I may not inherit a $360 million hotel chain, but I have sense enough to know that (in the most famous Paris pronouncement) Wal-Mart doesn't "like, uh, just sell walls."

Nicole is clearly the second banana in this show, and I'm waiting for the poor thing to figure that out. She's Gilligan to Paris's Skipper. I fully expect Paris to grab Nicole's hat and hit her over the head with it repeatedly. Nicole is the noxious wind beneath Paris's wings, limited to sighing and squealing as soon as she sees Paris sigh or squeal. The scene in which both girls recoil at the notion of plucking a chicken while Arkansas granny just shakes her head and huffs about the layabout Hollywood harlots is simply television at its finest.

Paris, whose nudie video continues to cause a stir, likes to visit the local eight-aisle Superette wearing jeans cut so low that she resembles a plumber more than a runway model. Classy!

In the earliest episodes, there appeared to be some small amount of chemistry between the Justin Timberlake–ish oldest brother in the host family and Paris, who is obsessed with discovering new ways to expose her "coin slot."

So, yes, we watch this show because it makes us feel good. We may never have enough money to casually spend $1,500 on a Gucci dog carrier like Paris (and one wonders if she really wants to buy a Nicole carrier for her little hanger-on buddy), but we can drive a straight shift without ripping the transmission out.

Yeah, we can.

Of course, some reality TV is too bad even to enjoy as a guilty pleasure. I'm thinking about the sincerely awful vehicle featuring Monica Lewinsky as the perky/wise hostess of a romantic reality and dating show. Yes, that's right. Monica Lewinsky dispensing dating advice to the lovelorn.

I was hoping we'd seen the last of the D.C. strumpet when she tearfully ran off the set of her own HBO special and into the arms of her Nutter Butter–brained mama, but nooooo. Monica has grabbed her fifteen minutes of fame, wrassled them to the ground, and is holding them—and us—hostage. She, like a bad burrito, simply won't go away.

Who can we blame for Monica's TV show, *Mr. Personality*? Could it beeee Satan? No, but you're close: the Fox Network.

In Episode One, an attractive stockbroker named Hayley must choose her ideal date from among twenty masked men. Get it? She can't see what they look like, so the guys must rely on their personalities to win her over. Personally,

I'm pulling for the troll with the one eye in the center of his forehead. As we say in the South, that oughta learn her.

Fox, in its own twisted way, probably thought the show was actually virtuous, even high-minded. After all, female contestants would be forced to date a guy based on his inner beauty.

Memo to Fox: Any guy with even an ounce of "inner beauty" wouldn't participate in this dreck.

As hostess, it would be Monica's job to act as Hayley's confidante, sharing dating advice.

If only I had had a chance to take Hayley aside, I would've told her that I know it's been a bad year for stockbrokers. (I know this because I just got the quarterly statement for my ever-dwindling 401-Kiss my money good-bye Plan and have spent most of the year mapping out a Fancy Feast retirement with my own Mr. Personality.)

But, girl, please. You do not want to take dating advice from Monica Lewinsky. Perhaps you've forgotten: Monica didn't get the guy. What's your next move? Acting classes from Mariah Carey?

Seeing Monica back in the news after so much time reminded me of a theory that I have about her: She is really an Osmond. No, really. The big black hair, the chipmunk cheeks, the Chiclets teeth. She is the Missing Osmond, the one they never talk about. The, as Donnie might say, "one bad apple."

Monica says her new job shouldn't surprise people. She

told *Newsweek* that her affair with President Clinton had made her a public figure and, "I've come to realize that I've already had my own reality show."

I can't see how to make this any tawdrier unless Fox makes Monica wolf a bowl of wriggling beetle larvae at the end of every show.

Memo to Fox: Settle down. I thought of it first.

The best reality shows are the ones that feature ordinary people. How much do we really want to watch of Farrah Fawcett carping at her bloated boyfriend, Ryan O'Neal? Give me *The Amazing Race* any day.

The thing that blows my mind is how many people will do anything to get on TV.

I have spent hours I can never get back watching TLC's trademark shows: *A Dating Story, A Wedding Story, A Baby Story,* and the like, and I can only hope that a *He Cheated and Now I'm Divorcing His Triflin' Ass Story* is in the works.

One of TLC's most popular shows is *What Not to Wear,* and, hons, it's as mean as Star Jones on Day Five of the Atkins Diet.

The premise is creepsome. Two "celebrity stylists" watch videotapes of women who dress poorly that have been *supplied by their friends and families.* (More on this later.) The stylists then confront the justifiably horrified bad dresser as she weeps into her plaid poncho with pom-poms, circa 1977, and promises to try to dress better, with their help.

The "stylists" have changed over the years. In the first

season, the show starred a flamboyant Fabio-haired Wayne Scot Lukas, who played off the diminutive and chatty Stacy London.

Mr. Lukas, who has since left the show, favored a signature look that mixed puka shells and buckskins. On camera, he was too easily distracted by the beauty of his own hair and spent much of the show flipping and tossing it about like a rather hard-faced Breck girl. In an interview, he explained that the show's important because "We all have body issues and all of our body issues are huge and all of our body issues are secrets."

Say what?

Stacy, who remains on the show with the milquetoast Clinton Somebody, dresses well enough but is as annoying as nail fungus with her constant squeals of "Shut *up!*" She says the show is all about confronting one's lack of style.

Or as Wayne Scot once put it, "When me and Stacy get you naked in a room, and we say, 'What do you hate about your body?' When they have to say it, their world crumbles."

As we vacuum the remnants of shattered self-esteem off the dressing room floor, let's consider the show's real villains, the family and "friends" who supply the humiliating videos of dear ol' Mom wearing her beloved fuzzy housecoat and bunny slippers in the privacy (ha-ha!) of her own home.

Reality TV is addictive, though. How else do you explain this disappointing vignette of my married life?

Not long ago, there was a moving and provocative documentary on PBS that detailed, in a most compelling way, the horrible racial strife in 1950s Mississippi. I knew it would be excellent, the kind of programming that makes even the no-TV nuts get their heads out of their subtitled "films" and rethink their position.

Of course, I didn't watch it. I had to see *Joe Millionaire,* in which a muscle-bound and rather vacant cutie pie courts greedy women who *think* he's a millionaire when, in fact, he's a bulldozer operator.

Oh, hons, I am *so* ashamed.

Joe Millionaire? My husband walked through the living room just as I flipped to the documentary so he'd think I was smart instead of the kind of person who secretly enjoys those awful fat baby shows on *Maury* and *Dr. Phil.* (And speaking of which, am I the only one to make the fat baby–fat mama connection? Hell-oooo.)

But I flipped channels too late. I was so busted. The moment had that kind of awful shame attached to it that is usually reserved for wolfing the last piece of cold pizza over the sink (where calories never count).

"Joe Millionaire?" he said. His tone hovered somewhere between disapproval and pity. I guess he felt like Connie Chung, who probably tells her girlfriends, "I thought I was

marrying a serious journalist, and now he has this show where he has contests to see who can pull the fat baby off the tricycle. I can hardly hold my head up at the network correspondents' dinner every year."

What is wrong with me? With our nation? Why, during a sneak preview of Fox's *Bridezilla,* which follows the weddings of the nation's most whiniest bitches, did I think, "Oh, baby, I am *so* TiVo-ing that."

Or Fox's *High School Reunion.* Typically, Fox likes lots of skin, so they plan to keep reunions to ten years, instead of, say, thirty, when it's doubtful anyone wants to bounce around the hot tub in a thong and conversations might revolve around who drove what route to get there and how steel-cut oatmeal had turned their lives and colons around.

Taking a tip from Fox, NBC's *Fear Factor* selects only female contestants with exceedingly large fake breasts and no measurable amount of body fat. These women are the kind who can convincingly make suggestive comments while devouring a plate of pig rectum. Hey, it's a gift.

I'm not proud of my viewing habits, but I can quit anytime I like. Well. Almost anytime. Dr. Phil has a 180-pound two-year-old toddler coming up, and I think he's looking for a wife.

15

Does Addiction to "Days of Our Lives" Mean That I Don't Actually Have One?

(A Life, That Is)

It's time to fess up: I have been imprisoned by a serious addiction for more than twenty-five years. The prison is in effect only from 1 to 2 p.m. Eastern Standard Time, but still.

My addiction to the idiotic *Days of Our Lives* is hugely embarrassing. I mean on the order of the time I had a big fight with my bank and emerged victorious only to discover that I had spinach glued to *every single one of my teeth*. Damn those veggie burritos.

Anyway, yes, I know that it is a stupid, stupid TV show full of cardboard cutout characters and poorly acted "plots." No matter. I find *Days* as irresistible as Horton family matriarch Grandma Alice's homemade doughnuts, which the poor ol' thing trots out for weddings, funerals, and serial killings.

HOPE BRADY: Gran, the Salem serial killer has just struck again! My father, my mother-in-law, and my stepfather-in-law are all dead!

MRS. H.: Have another doughnut, dear.

But, lately, something strange has been happening on *Days:* It's gotten interesting.

See, the serial killer who is killing off the cast one by one, sometimes as many as two a week, is none other than Salem's most esteemed psychiatrist, Dr. Marlena Evans, the sincere-faced long-legged beauty who has been the heart and soul of this show for decades.

Marlena—Doc to us—has counseled all of Salem at one time or the other, and now she's, *ick,* stabbing them with a letter opener to the carotid, outsmarting her buddies who spend much of every show saying, "We're going to get the killer. This won't happen again," but before we even go to a commercial break, oopsie, there's another body.

Truthfully, most victims have been, well, expendable. I was mildly miffed when she killed her ex-husband, Roman Brady, on his wedding day. I was hoping Roman would find true happiness with reformed whore Kate Roberts, but no.

After murdering him at his wedding reception, Marlena even comforted the grieving sorta-widow, patting her and offering the earnest-faced consolation we've come to expect.

Marlena's especially good at killing the goodhearted, dull ones like Caroline Brady and Doug Williams.

Doug was one-half of the famous DougandJulie, long-time annoying *Days* soul mates. I think they signed their checks just like that: DougandJulie. (True story: Back in the '80s, I entered a contest to win breakfast with the actors who play DougandJulie and won! They were lovely and boring just like on the show. I think I asked Doug if I could have the rest of his hash browns, and he said, "I guess.")

I know Doc's going to get caught, but it won't be anytime soon. The only one who's figured out it's Marlena is nineteen-year-old Sean, who's dating Doc's daughter, Belle, Salem's only virgin.

"Let the police handle this, son," said Sean's idiot cop father. But his cell phone crackles alive: "Oh, no! Another body!"

And time for another doughnut.

Sadly, I was forced to go cold turkey for two weeks without seeing *Days* when it was preempted by the Olympics.

Sure, you think that's pathetic, but that's just because you don't watch it. Otherwise you'd know that you can't expect people to just go on with their lives like normal when the last episode was a cliffhanger with Jennifer out there having a baby in the wilderness, Sean busting out of the house where he's been held prisoner by a psychotic wannabe girlfriend, and don't even get me started about Marlena and Roman (miraculously alive again!) making out in the jungle while his foot gets more gangrenous by the second. On top of that, Mimi thinks she's got cancer, Uncle

Mickey, 106, is gettin' some from a barmaid, and Sami just found out that her mama clawed her way out of her coffin. (You gotta love a show where the character says with a note of superiority and utter calmness, "See? I told you that Mom was buried alive, and you didn't even believe me.")

I get that it's unspeakably shallow to miss *Days* to the point of tears when the real heroes were over there in Greece, sprinting and wrestling and fencing and underwater-checkers playing and whatnot.

So I tried to really get into the Olympics and after I finally, sort of, succeeded, they ended. My life could resume, and I need never hear the painfully earnest preachings of the Rev. Bob Costas or see serious journalist Katie Couric giddily pretend to master the balance beam.

Low moment of viewing? When I simply didn't get the pole vault miscue and saw the woman sprint under the pole and told my husband, "Heck, I could do *that*."

Because I'm not a guy, I won't miss the barely there bikinis worn by the Olympic volleyball chicks. My husband says it has to do with wind resistance and improving their aerodynamic jumping abilities. He is so full of sand.

I think it has to do with them being hoochie mamas. Talented, sickeningly fit hoochie mamas, but hoochies nonetheless.

I came to the Olympics embarrassingly late and so missed the big ruckus caused by the American who won the gold, although it was later discovered, after the judges sobered up, that the guy from Taiwan was the rightful winner. There's a fascinating debate about this, but it's not nearly so fascinating as watching Bo Brady of *Days* try to decipher signals his kidnapped family is trying to transmit from a mysterious island.

Now *that's* gold-medal TV.

PART III

Vanity Flares

16

This Blonde Isn't as Dumb as You Think

Online IQ Test Proves I'm a Visionary
(Whatever the Hell That Is)

Probably the last people who are unapologetically joked about and ridiculed in public are blondes. People think we be stupid just because our hair is yeller, and they're not too shy to say so. Most folks think the average blonde doesn't know the difference between come 'ere and sic 'um.

If you don't believe it, consider that there are entire Web sites devoted to collecting and distributing dumb blonde jokes. Which reminds me, how many blondes does it take to change a lightbulb? Two. One to hold the Diet Coke and the other to call "Daaady!" I love that one.

Or this one: What do you call it when a blonde dyes her hair brunette? Artificial intelligence.

Har-dee-har-har.

The stereotype of the dumb blonde is as old as that, uh, really dark stuff that grass and trees and stuff grow in.

I started out blond. Then something strange happened in my thirties, and my hair started getting darker and darker. Call it hormones, call it genetics, call it really bad luck, but I knew immediately that I couldn't accept not being blond.

A trip to my beloved hairdresser, Brenda (pronounced "Branda" in the South), remedied the problem. It wasn't painless, my hons. No, far from it. Brenda tied a plastic rain bonnet tight on my head, then used what looked like a crochet hook to pull wisps of formerly blond hair through holes in the cap. I cried and flapped my hands and endured the pain, all in the name of being blond again. Finally, she zapped the wisps with purple goo, and two hours later, I was blonder than ever.

Naturally, I was ecstatic, but as y'all know, a few weeks later, I was *Roots: The Next Generation*. It was horrible realizing that this would have to be an ongoing process. So, for the past fifteen years, I've faithfully trotted to Brenda, who now, mercifully, uses little foil strips.

All that said, imagine my shock when Britney Spears, our national spokesmodel for all things blond, decided to go brunette, literally and figuratively returning to her roots. One week, she's blond as God and Preference by L'Oréal intended and doing things like marrying and divorcing in a day, and the next, she dyes her hair, becomes a brunette, and starts studying Jewish mysticism.

On behalf of blondes everywhere, what up?

Oh, Britney, must we turn to Christina Applegate or—horrors!—Courtney Love as our leader now?

As a blonde in mind, spirit, and bottle, I'm not worried. The ability to do math and chew gum at the same time is highly overrated. Britney'll be back.

As if losing my blondeness isn't bad enough, lately something strange has been happening with my eyeballs.

For a year or so now, I've gotten lots of snickers from friends who think it's odd that I read my menu at arm's length.

"Arms too short?" Heh, heh, heh.

"Isn't it time you got some reading glasses?"

"The same thing happened to my eyes when I turned fifty."

Fifty?!

I'm not fifty, although I can sort of make it out as a blurry image in the not-so-distant future. Yes, yes, I realize that "getting older beats the alternative," but I am a vain creature.

When I recently asked the waiter at a fancy restaurant for a pair of "house reading glasses," he looked at me with the same disdain as if I had asked for a foam doughnut to sit on.

My friend who is a little younger than me recently had a miniature nervous breakdown after a department store clerk cheerily deducted an extra 15 percent "because today is Senior Day!"

"What does that have to do with me?" my friend asked innocently, still not understanding the full horror of what had been bestowed on her forty-two-year-old self.

"Well," continued the smiling and clueless clerk, "see, on Tuesday, everybody fifty-five or older gets an additional discount!"

"You think I'm fifty-five?" she asked, an edge of hysteria creeping into her voice.

"Well, uh, uh, well."

Although I haven't been offered the Senior Day discount, I have experienced a sad, nostalgic tug as the grocery store clerk doesn't even bother to look up to okay my wine purchase.

Oh, of course, I don't look twenty-one, or even double that, but it would just be so much fun if she would falter, just for a nanosecond, before punching the override key.

When it's time to write the check and I fumble for the reading glasses that now live in the bottom of my purse in complete denial, I could swear she sighs and rolls her eyes.

Not long ago, as I stood in the grocery line, a nice man in his seventies, I'd guess, noticed my giggling six-year-old as she completed the joyous task of choosing between Gummi Savers and Nerds.

"Lord-a-mercy, don't we love our grands!" he said with a kindly chuckle.

I thought he meant the biscuits, so I nodded enthusiastically. I was halfway to my car with the bag boy ("Ma'am, do you need help with that? I mean what *is* your bone density these days?") before the full impact hit. Grands? *Grands?* Bring on the Botox, hons. I'm not going down without a fight.

The awful truth is that, if I have to choose between being a dumb cute blonde or a smart mousy brown, I'm going with cute every time. Fortunately, I don't have to choose. Although I've always thought that smarts-wise, I'm somewhere between the two Simpsons—Jessica and Marge—it turns out I'm a genius.

At least that's what the on-line IQ test I took said.

It turns out that there are like a million of these on-line IQ tests out there in cyberspace. (That's ten hundred thousand to the rest of you.) Some are sponsored by Mensa, the worldwide organization of smart people. In my experience, Mensans tend to be a bit belligerent about how smart they are. (I say belligerent, but I could also have said haughty, pugnacious, or quarrelsome. See how smart I is?) They're also disproportionately fond of medieval fairs and *Star Trek* conventions and living in their mamas' basements.

So, anywho, I took the IQ test, and guess what? I'm, like, a *genius!* Right. I already told you that. Okay, technically, they didn't use the G-word once my score was computed, but they did say that I fit the profile of a "visionary philosopher." Well, roll me up and call me curly! Who knew?

I was so excited with my score (it's tacky to brag, but let's just say it was in the, ahem, 140s) that I shoved the printout under hubby's nose at breakfast the next morning.

"Read it and sleep," I said triumphantly.

"You mean weep?" he asked.

"Whatever."

So he read the analysis and damned near choked on his Cheerios when he read the part about me having "a powerful mix of skills and insight, like Plato."

"You sure they don't mean Pluto?" he joked.

Now wasn't that an odious, repugnant thing to say?

I suppose the reason he questioned my test results was a single sentence that referred to my "exceptional math and verbal skills."

This phrase did not have the ring of verisimilitude because I am famously bad at math. If I'm in charge of tipping at a restaurant, the waiter will either fall to his knees in gratitude or slash my tires. There ain't no Mr. In Between.

The results of my IQ test said that as a visionary philosopher, I can "anticipate and predict patterns." It's so true. Don't I know, instinctively, every time the clearance at Stein Mart is going to jump from 50 to 75 percent? It's God-given; you can't learn it.

You're probably worried that, from now on, I'm going to write about just boring visionary stuff, but I'm not. One must bloom where one is planted. I think Pluto said that.

17

The Butcher's Great, the Baker's Suffering

But How Is the Anti-Carb Frenzy Affecting the Candlestick Maker?

It's official. Every human being I know is now on the Atkins Diet. Sure, they look kind of silly, sitting there eating puddles of spaghetti sauce without the noodles underneath like God and Emeril intended, but they're *serious*. No side of garlic bread for them. But, yes, please, another eight-pound meatball!

Like most women my age who eat a lot of fudge and don't exercise, I've gained a bit of weight recently, and so I decided that the Atkins Diet was worth a try. Any diet that encourages mass consumption of T-bones and kielbasa sausages can't be all bad, right?

Wrong. I lasted exactly thirty-two hours on the Atkins Diet and have no intentions of ever trying it again. Without carbohydrates—and lots of them—I discovered that I really did have the capacity to take another's life. And *enjoy* it.

Particularly if the "other" was eating a big, fat yeast roll in front of me. In which case we would, once again, trot out the "but, Yer Honor, he needed killin' " defense so popular in our South.

Carbohydrates, from the Latin, *carbo* which means "yummy" and *hydrates* which means "cinnamon bun," are not something I can eliminate or even drastically cut back on.

There is no joy in a steak without a baked potato, a hot dog without a bun, a casserole without noodles, a movie starring Jimmy Fallon.

The late Dr. Atkins believed that restricting carbs would cause the body to burn up its stored fat faster. Ha! That might work for most people, but I can assure you that my body, in thirty-two hours, was already plotting new and more embarrassing places to store fat.

I don't dispute that the Atkins Diet works for most people. I've seen women shed fifty pounds in a matter of weeks using this diet. The only bad part is that if you slip up and eat, say, a single French fry or a saltine, you will wake up twenty pounds heavier. It's cruel that way.

Weight Watchers makes more sense to me, and that would be my first choice of diets except they assign "points" to food, and this involves a lot of math, calculating the dietary fat grams divided by the calories and then converting it all into these "points."

According to WW, I am entitled to a measly 23 points a day but I'd use up 18 of them in just one order of Taco Bell's Nachos Bell Grande, or, as I like to call it, heaven on a cardboard plate.

The South Beach Diet is similar to the Atkins Diet in that carbs are a huge no-no in the beginning. Bill Clinton lost lots of weight on the South Beach Diet, but then he had heart bypass surgery, so I'm not so sure about it. Also, South Beach has a *lot* of rules. The book weighs, like, eight tons or so. I think most South Beachers lose the weight not by following all the instructions so carefully but simply by lugging that stupid book around.

The Zone delivers steady weight loss that's not so quick or so visible as Atkins and South Beach, but it also has a lot of rules, and the supplements and exotic Zone-sanctioned meals (fillet of froufrou with a side of pistachio-encrusted doodahs) ain't cheap. The Zone believes that you can best lose weight if you balance protein and carbs in a 40–30–30 mix. That's 40 percent protein, 30 percent carbs, and 30 percent of something else that I can't remember, so just substitute fried Snickers bars for that one.

With all these diets around, we've all become completely carb-phobic. The other day, I was in Subway eating my favorite Jared-sanctioned six-inch veggie on whole wheat when a rather portly *total stranger* walked up and asked, "Do you realize how many CARBS are in that thing?"

He couldn't have looked more horrified if I'd been sitting there eating a shit sandwich. He then took a seat across the aisle from me and unwrapped what appeared to be turkey, bacon, ham, pepperoni, and a leg of lamb all wrapped up in a strange little scrap of brown crepe so thin you could read your Atkins Diet book through it.

One after another, customers came in and ordered "Atkins sauce" on their "sandwiches." I can only imagine that this is actual blood from a meat-producing animal.

The thing about Atkinsians is that they are a trifle high and mighty, aren't they? "Oh, I can't eat that. I'm doing Atkins!" Don't get so uppity, fool. It's not like you're becoming a missionary or something.

A waiter friend says he's regularly berated by women who scream "Get that out of here!" I mean it's hot bread, not a rabid possum, he's bringing to the table with cute little shell-shaped butter pats on a doily.

The stranger who had criticized my veggie sub finished his whatever-it-was and stopped by my table to tell me that his mother—*his mother*—was about my age, and she was losing a lot of weight with Atkins.

Okay, here's the thing. Don't assume that a woman is on a diet. My husband likes me just the way I am. He points out that he doesn't have to "shake the sheets to find me," and that's the way it's going to stay.

The Atkins lingo is confusing, too.

"We're in the induction phase now," a friend confided over two pounds of bacon the other morning.

"I'm so sorry," I said, missing her meaning. "But y'all can try again or even get a surrogate."

What the hell are they talking about?

Carbohydrates have become the new embodiment of evil. Did you know that if you rearrange the letters in the word *Carbohydrate,* it spells "Cameron Diaz can't act"? Yeah, I know I made it up, but that's what we crazy carbmonsters do. We lie! Don't blame us: It's the gluten. Makes a girl do strange things.

Men and women both diet, of course, but men don't take it as seriously as we do. My friend Lisa came home from work the other day to a horrific sight.

There was her loving husband, still wearing his suit and tie from work, holding a just-opened bottle of Miller Lite and . . . weighing himself.

That's right. Standing on the scales in front of God and everybody, *casually* checking his weight at the end of the day.

"What are you *doing?*" Lisa shrieked.

Her husband looked at her curiously, as if she were, somehow, the crazy one. Then he cocked his head a bit, which as every woman knows, can actually make you weigh three ounces more.

"I'm checking my weight," he said. "Something wrong?"

Oh, yes, my friend. Something is very, very wrong. No

woman on the face of the earth would actually stand, fully dressed at the end of the day, on a set of scales. I mean besides Renée Zellweger, who, let's face it, practically has HELP ME! scrawled across her bony little chest these days.

For Lisa's husband to weigh himself while holding a beer is too much to bear. Might as well spit into my "burns more fat" yogurt.

Women know that there are some essential guidelines to the proper weigh-in. For starters, you weigh only in the morning, before breakfast and after all bodily functions have been attended to. Women weigh after flossing, Q-tipping their ears, and even blowing their noses. Every possible source of added weight must be eliminated.

Also, and this should go without saying, you have to weigh yourself buck nekkid. I have seen grown, professional women (okay, me) sob in protest at stepping on a doctor's office scale while fully clothed.

ME: This dress is heavily beaded; you'll need to deduct at least twelve pounds.

NURSE: I don't see any beads.

ME: What are you? The frickin' *bead police?*

So I told my husband about Lisa's insensitive lout of a husband, but he didn't get it. "What's the big deal with women and weight? I mean, why are you so worried? What do you weigh, anyway? One twenty? One twenty-five?"

Suddenly, I felt much better. "Yes," I said. Well. Maybe in outer space.

18

Fashion Forecast

Run, Run Rudolph, Nipple Jewelry for Morons, and Get Thee a Behind, You!

My closest friends have warned me that I don't have the guts to write about this subject, but that's what they said when I wrote about artificial testicles for neutered dogs, so who's laughing now? Well, probably not the dogs.

A dedicated humor writer doesn't shy away from the tough stories, the ones that might even make a few enemies. And that's why it's time to take on a subject that is hallowed to many women, even a religion of sorts. I speak, of course, of the holiday sweater cult.

Those of you who are reading this whilst fingering the delicate silver bells attached to the meticulously embroidered reindeer tableau that is dancing across your chest might want to bail now.

I never noticed the cult until my daughter started

kindergarten, although I'm not a big fan of "character wear" in general. There's just something not quite right about those grown women who wear Tweety Bird sweatshirts over their leggings at the mall. I mean unless you run a daycare center, isn't it time to move on and get Road Runner off your chest? And nobody over the age of ten should ever wear any article of clothing that announces I TAWT I TAW A PUDDYTAT. Talk about a cry for help.

But I digress. It's the holiday sweater cult that has got me in a swivet. At the kindergarten Fall Festival, I apparently didn't get the memo that I must wear an elegant themed sweater painstakingly adorned with pumpkins, ghosts, and bats.

Some of these sweaters are insanely expensive. One cult member confided to me that she once spent $250 for a butter-soft wool sweater with dancing candy canes and nutcrackers prancing around her neck. Her eyes danced, her voice became high-pitched—she wanted me to drink the Kool-Aid, no question.

Class wars are evident. You've got your $14.98 Frosty the Snowman from Wal-Mart versus your $200 Brighton version from the prissy boutique with the size 0 sales staff, and don't think the cult members won't know the difference.

Far be it from me to question another's sense of fashion (I did, after all, wear a mod paper dress in junior high during an unfortunate Carnaby Street phase) but this whole cutesy-wootsy, elves-are-eating-my-brain thing where you own an entire wardrobe of sweaters with buttons that can be pushed to play "The Twelve Days of Christmas" is beyond me.

One friend told me she has enough sweaters to wear a different Christmas sweater from December first to twenty-fifth. My only response was, "Why?"

Fashion is a hobby for me. I'm fascinated by women who spend five hundred dollars on a single pair of high heels. Even if I had that kind of dough, I wouldn't do it, because somewhere in the back of my noggin sits Sally Struthers pitifully imploring me to "Please help Save the Children." (And the awful, shameful me always thinking, *Whoa, Sally, if you'd ease up on the Toaster Strudels, you could save a few right there.*)

So, no, I can't spend five hundred dollars for shoes. Guess I'm just too much of a hick. Here's another confession: I don't own a single piece of nipple jewelry.

I read recently where Janet Jackson's personal stylist spent hours perusing nipple jewelry before he found that now-legendary sunburst design that was revealed during the Super Bowl halftime show.

Who the hell has enough money to hire someone to shop for her nipple jewelry? It makes me feel downright dowdy for getting excited about finally buying one of those shirts with my initial on it. Shopping for nipple jewelry? Doesn't Janet ever need just, you know, socks?

My daughter, a huge Justin Timberlake fan who even has a little silver 'N Sync cell phone that is programmed to call her and say good night every night from J. T. himself, was eager to watch the Super Bowl halftime show.

So while hubby showered, as he does during all Super Bowl halftime shows, even if we're at other people's houses (what can I say—the man hates pageantry), the princess and I settled in to see her beloved Justin perform.

I like to consider myself a modern mom, capable of handling discussions of sex and stuff without blushing and flapping. Still, I was unprepared for the big rip-off. I stopped my Dorito in midcrunch. What was that?

I didn't even notice the, uh, boob. I was wondering what that thing was attached to it, and I don't mean Justin's paw.

"Mommy," pondered Precious, "why did Justin rip that lady's top off?"

Channeling the wisdom of my foremothers (who am I kidding—all they had to worry about was not dying in childbirth, making homemade soap out of cow ear wax, and doing the nasty in the same bed where your eleven children are trying to sleep), I decided to answer her question honestly.

"Ratings, sugar. It's all about shock and awe, corporate greed, and a culture that is increasingly morally challenged."

"You talk funny, Mommy."

All was forgiven that night when her 'N Sync phone rang right at bedtime with a cheery "Sleep tight, and don't let the bedbugs bite!" from Justin. Amazing how he can do all that *and* find time to expose Janet Jackson's dinners on national television.

Thank heavens the NFL issued an official statement condemning the halftime show antics as "embarrassing, offensive, and inappropriate" and all but called for its smelling salts and shawl. I can only assume that this means that from now on, all NFL cheerleaders will be wearing burkas and shimmying only slightly suggestively.

Right. That'll happen.

All I want is for someone to please tell Janet Jackson where Talbots is.

She might want to focus on another part of her admittedly buff body. According to fashion insiders, "The boob, it's been done. It's old, but the butt is new!" Only fashionistas can say something like that without cracking themselves up.

What are they talking about? Buttocks cleavage, you fashion Neanderthal. BC is taking over the nation. Open your eyes and see for yourself. The look once popularized by jovial plumbers everywhere is now hotter 'n fish grease.

Not blessed with an audacious onion? Fear not, Jane Hathaway! Buttocks implants are the new must-have accessory for the true fashionista. Just ask Paris Hilton. But remember to speak very slowly.

In case you still don't get the picture, let plastic surgeon Bruce Nadler of New York City explain it to you: "You want two mounds that are very discrete so you have a valley in between them. It's like having the perfect push-up bra," except for the fact that it's on your ass.

This is all, of course, another example of plastic surgery following fashion. All those low-rise jeans out there, the ones with the quarter-inch-long zippers, means a lot of butt gets exposed in the process. With surgery, you can actually have your butt puffed up to make rear-end cleavage to keep your pants more interesting. I know! I know! I'm dizzy with the possibilities myself!

It should be only a matter of time before the "front butt" look popularized by overweight women who prefer very tight pants while cruising the aisles of Wal-Mart becomes the new must-have accessory. ("You wanna see some front butt, honey? When I wear my orange stretch capris, you can't tell whether I'm a-comin' or a-goin'!")

To go along with all this low-rise, puffed-up-butt trend, you'll want to add a very large tattoo. Turns out that a tattoo that shows just, like, the top third of an eagle, sunset, or some such before disappearing into the jeans completes the look. As explained by one excited New York tattoo artist, "The lower back is what the ankle was!"

Okay, let's see if I got this straight. The butt is the new breast, and the lower back is the new ankle. Now if only we could figure out where the brain has moved.

19

Ass-Lifting, Face-Tightening, Boob-Bustin' Products

Right On or Rip-Off? You'll Have to Ask My Pantyhose

I hate to admit it, but *The Swan* has gotten inside my head, and I can't get it out. Every time I look in my mirror, I hear the velvety voice of the hit reality TV show's fancy-pants Beverly Hills plastic surgeon saying, "She will, of course, need a brow lift, upper and lower face lift, liposuction on the cheeks, buttocks, chin, inner and outer thighs, calves, ankles, and eyelids, breast augmentation, nose job, tummy tuck, gum tissue recontouring, Zoom bleaching, dental veneers, a lip lift, hair extensions, and—oh what the hell—a brand new head."

I know that *The Swan* has made a lot of thoughtful people ponder the disturbing shallowness of a culture that pursues, at all costs, some random notion of "beauty." But not being a thoughtful person, it just made me wonder if I shouldn't apply for the next installment.

The only bad part would be that *Swan* contestants are allowed only three ten-minute phone calls home a week for four months. That's not nearly enough time to explain, in painstaking detail once again, where I "hide" the laundry detergent (on the shelf above the washer—call me devil-may-care!) or the princess's SpongeBob macaroni and cheese (the pantry!) or, naturally, the car keys.

One of the biggest complaints critics of *The Swan* have is that the show deliberately selects sad sacks with zero self-esteem just to boost ratings. Hons, that's just good storytelling, if you ask me. When one aspiring *Swan* was being wheeled into a seven-hour surgery, she tried three times to call her husband for a few last-minute words of encouragement only to be told he was on a smoke break.

Ewww.

On the final night, when an ultimate Swan was crowned, I had a chance to look at the husbands, who were all in the range from extremely ordinary to butt ugly. Of course, it was a little hard to see through the veneer of drool during the cheesy lingerie competition, when the contestants trotted out their new "full D" figures.

It was some consolation that pageant winner Rachel Love-Fraser chose not to enhance her smallish bust, a curiously satisfying victory for those of us who just dream of being a "full A."

Lest you think Fox was insensitive to every need of these women, consider that they hired a "life coach" to help counsel the women during their four months of mirrorless isolation.

Still, I was underwhelmed by Coach Nely Galan's approach to at least one weepy and bandage-wrapped contestant: "Do you realize how many people would love to have this chance? I'm honestly disappointed that you're not trying harder."

Like they say, with a life coach like that, who needs flesh-eating bacteria?

We women do crazy things to make sure that we look our best.

My friend Patsy Jo is getting ready to attend her thirtieth high school reunion, and she has prepared for it in a sane and sensible way: She has ordered Face Lift in a Bottle.

Apparently you paint the stuff on your face, and the goo has a tightening, lifting effect that makes you look years younger. The only thing is, it lasts only about six hours, so you could be taut and fabulous at cocktail hour and seem to have aged horribly by the end of dessert.

I'd like to try it for my next reunion, but I'm afraid I'd screw up the application and come out looking like a cross between Joan Rivers and the Elephant Man. Or I'd use too much and end up looking like one of those raku crackle pots.

Although I'd never heard of Face Lift in a Bottle, I have tried a few beautifying remedies of my own that smacked of quackery. The weirdest one was something called the Amazing Disappearing Double Chin-Strap, a sweaty band of very tight latex that you strapped on in hopes of eliminating the dreaded midlife double chin. The ads made it sound so easy: "Wear Amazing Disappearing Double Chin-Strap while you do your household chores!"

Friends who dropped by were treated to quite a sight. "What *happened?*" they'd shriek. "Were you in a car wreck?"

"No, silly!" I would say. "It's going to get rid of my double chin."

Actually, I had to sign most answers because my lips had been pushed up to my nose, making normal conversation difficult.

After weeks of faithfully wearing the gizmo, I had to admit there was no difference, and I tossed it. The only good news was that I could finally stop doing household chores.

There was also a failed experiment in do-it-yourself breast augmentation. I have a number of friends who have gotten boob jobs from a licensed plastic surgeon, but that stuff costs money. Nope, I decided I would try Beauti-Breast instead. The way it works is that you place your tatas inside two funnel-shaped cups that attach to "any household faucet or spigot." (I don't know the difference either, except I think spigots are usually outside, and this was definitely not going to be something I did in my driveway.)

Once hooked up, you turned on the water and, according to "scientific research," the tremendous volume of water shooting through the funnels would somehow lead to what scientists refer to as "really big tits."

It was a rip-off, of course. It would've been much cheaper to strap myself, topless, to the hood of my car next time it went through the Auto Spa.

All this just proves there is no magic fountain—or even spigot—of youth and beauty, sister-hons. Only through rest, exercise, and healthy diet can we help ourselves look our best.

I know; I crack myself up.

The latest national beauty obsession is to have teeth so bright that we can use them to read at night. ("Aim your choppers over here, Martha, I can't see the *TV Guide* cross-word.")

Don't get me wrong. I like white teeth as much as the next person. Someday, I even hope to own some, although there's a better than even chance that they'll be the kind that must sit, grinning maniacally, from the confines of a watery glass beside my bed.

The real thing just seems like too much work. For example, those ubiquitous whitening strips that brag that you can discreetly brighten your smile while you go about your life, even while working out! But I don't want to work out. Do they have any that work if you just want to sit on your ass and watch *Judging Amy*?

"I'm getting a whiter smile," says the smarty-pants spokesmodel on the commercial, as she, like, jumps from a plane or something else more exciting than my typical day: folding laundry while simultaneously eating the last of the mini-Snickers from Halloween.

People have become so obsessed with whiter teeth that those of us who don't use strips, gels, brush-ons, and trays are starting to look like Austin Powers in comparison.

I actually met a young woman the other day whose teeth were so white, they were blue.

"Your teeth are amazing," I said, though it was hard for her to hear me because I was speaking from behind my hand, suddenly ashamed of my own teeth, less knockout than Niblets.

"I know," she said, smiling even wider.

"I think you just put my eyes out."

A check of some of the teeth-whitening products out there reveals that you can actually get your teeth eleven shades whiter if you have them professionally bleached. Eleven shades! What are they using? Clorox? I think I'll take my wine-stained best tablecloth to the dentist next time I go.

Recently, I read a testimonial for a professional bleaching product from a young couple who spent the month before their wedding getting their teeth custom-bleached so their smiles would match on their big day. Haven't these idiots ever heard of Photoshop? Hons, if I got married today, I'd have those wedding photos shave off my hips, whiten my smile, and give me the bust that I have so richly deserved all my life.

And to think, the only thing we used to worry about was making sure the bridesmaids' dresses matched the punch.

Everything's so complicated now, what with all these products to make us gorgeous. Even the simple act of buying pantyhose is maddening. Gone are the days when you could just buy that little L'Eggs egg, size B, nude, sheer toe.

When I went pantyhose shopping recently, I discovered that a lot has happened, not much of it good.

Did I want pantyhose infused with microencapsulated caffeine or grapefruit scents?

No thanks. The way my thighs rub together, I'd smell like Starbucks all day, and that would just lead to me and everyone around me craving triple-fat mochaccinos, and then where would we all be? Size C, that's where.

The theory behind injecting grapefruit and caffeine into hosiery is that it makes it last longer, even after repeated washings. This is, to use the technical term, utter crap.

Some pantyhose boast of chemical additives to make you feel better as you walk. I'm guessing the nude, size B, Vicodin pantyhose are particularly popular with movie stars.

The rest of us must settle for pantyhose injected with things like "jojoba." I'm not sure what jojoba is, but I'm pretty sure I don't want it anywhere near my noonie.

I also discovered something called "bum boost" pantyhose by Pretty Polly for sagging buttocks. (And, yet again, I'm struck by what a terrific name that would be for a rock band: Sagging Buttocks.) This is great! Next time hubby asks why I'm acting like I have my ass on my shoulders, I can just smile and say, "I do, and it's all thanks to Pretty Polly!"

The most popular of the new breed of pantyhose promises to reduce cellulite. As you walk, tiny encapsulated anti-cellulite lotions are working to massage your dimpled thighs into smoothness. (See "utter crap," above.)

Look. Cellulite is a hereditary curse. Some friends and I once spent six months dutifully rolling our thighs with rolling pins every morning and evening to "break up the cellulite." It was a dismal failure, so we eventually came to our senses and went out for pie.

There's also "age-defying" pantyhose. Now this is exciting, indeed. I love the idea of defiant pantyhose getting themselves all worked up over every little thing. What's that, Officer? You think I was speeding? Well, let's just see what my pantyhose have to say about that, mister.

"Let your pantyhose work hard for you!" says the advertisement. I couldn't love this more. I'm taking a break and letting my new pantyhose write for a while.

As long as the caffeine's in 'em, they should do just fine.

The truth is, no matter how much we primp and preen and how much we spend on cosmetics (I once accidentally spent forty-eight dollars for a La Prairie lip gloss and, trust me, this is nothing Laura Ingalls Wilder ever used), you're still going to have spinach-teeth or, in my case, a third breast.

When you have a book published, a funny thing happens: People who know perfectly well that you write for a living suddenly expect you to also be able to do radio and TV shows, spin plates on a stick, whatever! Writers are used to working alone. We sit around in our pajamas, watching the world go by from a small upstairs home office whose windows really need cleaning and whose psychedelic curtains that seemed so cool five years ago now look stupid, like Marilyn Manson's idea of a nursery window topper.

To push your book, you must do dozens of radio and TV shows. Recently, while being interviewed on a half-hour TV show, I thought things were going swimmingly until, during the break, one of the cameramen walked over and said, "Uh, could you adjust your shirt? It kinda looks like you got a third breast in there."

Okay, so *now* I'm completely relaxed. While my jaw drops at this horrible revelation, I hear the host say cheerily, "And we're back!" The camera cuts to me, but I can't be bothered. Suddenly, I'm pulling and jerking on my puckered sweater like it's a straitjacket. When the host asks a question, I don't even look up, just mumble, "Huh? Yeah, okay, just let me fix this."

And then there was the time that my cat fell asleep on my face (don't ask) and gave me poison ivy just two days before I was supposed to go on the road for a book tour.

This is incredibly ironic when you're telling everybody

that your book is called *We're Just Like You, Only Prettier*. Scratching my cheeks raw and covered in oozing red sores and patches of white calamine lotion, I made small children run from me. "Wait!" I cried. "Come back! I don't usually look like this. Come back! Wanna see my third breast?"

PART IV

Huzzzbands

20

The Paradoxical Male

Smart Enough to Find "Me Time," but Dumb Enough to Get Stuck Buying the Tampons

My husband took advantage of our state's "tax-free" week-end as only a man can. While I sat home clipping coupons to save seventy-five cents on Cinnamon Life cereal, he was out buying a computer, something called a wireless broad-band router (I have no idea), a PC bundle pack that in-cludes lots of stuff we already have, and . . . a shiny new bicycle!

You have to love that after a tough morning of computer buying, doggone it, he deserved some "me time" on his very own new bike. Men.

"I didn't know bikes qualified for tax-free," I huffed.

"Oh, it didn't," he said. "But it was so big and red and shiny."

Apparently lobotomies were on sale, too. Hubby then

explained that, thanks to his smart, tax-free shopping, we had actually saved $136 in sales tax.

Whoa, now. This is *my* argument, the old spend-money-to-save-money one that he always refutes when it comes to truly useful stuff like a butter-soft leather trench in teal that matches my eyes.

"There's more!" he said, practically dancing about the room. "There's a rebate on everything—well, except the bike, of course."

Oh, goody. Now I get to experience that particular circle of hell known as rebate redemption.

That afternoon, I gathered together the rebate forms, including lengthy rules for redemption, and a box cutter that would be used to either carve the original UPC from the boxes or to end my life, whichever seemed more appealing.

After an hour or so spent looking for the serial number for one product, I called the toll-free "rebate question hotline for doofuses." A computer-generated voice told me where to find it, and let's just say I felt pretty stupid, like the kind of person who couldn't find her serial number in the dark with both hands and a flashlight. It was right there in tiny print beneath the bottom quarter flap of the third perpendicular.

I wanted my mommy.

Next, I started to work with the box cutter to remove the UPCs. Except there were lots of them. Those little barcodes were everywhere, and they all looked different.

Which was the right one? Another call to the hotline resolved that, too—although was it my imagination or was the computerized voice growing impatient with me?

Finally, I needed a legible copy of the store sales receipt with appropriate items circled in ink, a copy of the ESN (who knows?), my college transcript, voter registration card, and Penney's bra-and-panty-club membership card.

Well, almost.

By nightfall, I'd driven to the copy shop twice and was only halfway through the paperwork. I needed help, but hubby had gone for a bike ride "to unwind."

Men just don't take things as seriously as women do. It's not just that we do all the rebates, Mother's Day gift-buying, and so on, but they just don't think anything's all that serious.

If you don't believe me, consider these two words: Hooters Air.

Men are the brains (sort of) behind the nation's newest and orangest airline. Up in those ultrafriendly skies, I'm guessing every cloud has a silicone lining.

Only a man could dream up an airplane full of attentive, buxom, chirpy Hooters girls wearing barely there tangerine hot pants serving drinks and snacks.

The "airline's" press people have been very careful to point out that, in the event of an emergency, you will not be expected to rely on a Hooters Girl to save your sorry self. That's right; not even by grabbing one to use as a flotation device, tempting as that might be.

The real flight attendants will be doing all the safety drills and such. Great. It's high school all over again, with the bookish, flat-chested women trying to get you to listen and respect us—er, them—while the cheerleader with the stupendous tatas is happily doing cartwheels in the background and getting all the attention.

What a Hooters Air passenger should hear: "Please place your tray tables in an upright and locked position."

What he does hear: "Hi, my name is Tawny, and I like spring mornings and newborn puppies."

So far, business is good—and it's no wonder. Whoever filed this business plan was no boob. Cheap fares, golf packages, *and* big balambas? That's like the holy trinity to most of the men I know. Throw in a bottomless bowl of Doritos, *SportsCenter* on the overhead TV monitors, and a case of Coronas, and you've pretty much got the recipe for Complete Male Bliss.

It's unlikely that Hooters Air, with its fleet of gently used 737s that are probably way older than the average Hooters Girl, will ever need to file for bankruptcy, unlike its snooty, humorless competition. I predict no need for a "federal bailout" or similar silliness.

I think that US Airways and the rest of the bankrupt airlines should take a lesson from Hooters Air. Stop taking yourselves so seriously with your "business class" and your blah-blah-blah endless CNN Headline News. Put a little fun back into flying. Pilots, show us some chiseled calf muscles!

There's something delightfully, guiltily un-PC about Hooters Air. Oh, sure, I know I'm supposed to be all offended and indignant (further objectifying women, what*ever*) but, try as I might, I can't even work up a mild, powdered-cappuccino froth on this one.

It's the same reaction I have to the annual slew of letters from outraged school librarians canceling subscriptions to *Sports Illustrated* after the swimsuit issue comes out. "Well, I never!" they always huff. Probably not. But I'll bet Tawny has.

Men aren't really pigs, of course. They just know what they want (see shiny red bike, above), and they aren't ashamed of it.

Men, as my husband continues to remind me, are extremely simple creatures. Still not convinced? Then maybe you need to read a study that found that male geniuses make their greatest scientific discoveries all because they want to get laid.

The study of male scientists has discovered that geniuses do their best work in their early thirties (before their brains shrivel to the size of a grape tomato) and that work stems from a need to impress a member of the opposite sex. *New Scientist* magazine reported that "the male competitive urge to attract females is a driving force for scientific achievements."

This explains why Albert Einstein, who, bless his heart, had a face that would stop a clock and raise hell with small watches, didn't sweat the personal grooming stuff. He knew that the way to get the babes was to, like, invent something. ("Won't go to the Scientists' Pot Luck Supper with me? Well, would you go with the inventor of the theory of relativity? I thought so.")

Louis Pasteur, famous for discovering a way to heat liquids to prevent the growth of bacteria, a process known as Louisization, I believe, was all in it for the babes, although his favorite pickup line could've used a little work. ("Come upstairs, and I'll show you an explosion of activity in my petri dishes!")

Jonas Salk was just another unmotivated Generation A'er until he discovered the vaccine for influenza while trying to attract the attentions of any future Mrs. Salks.

The study said that genius men (loosely defined as any man who can close a kitchen cabinet door) "do what they do to win the sexual attention of women."

Sure, it all seems less noble when you realize that all the genius scientists are out there fiddling with cancer cures just to score with the hot new girl scientist in the lab, but I say the end justifies the means.

If you put singer and lingerie model Kylie Minogue actually in the lab, we'd probably see a battle that would make *Freddy Vs. Jason* look like a meeting of the Women's Missionary Union.

Unfortunately, such hormone-driven genius doesn't last very long. The study found that, as the competitive drive decreases with age, men geniuses shift their priorities from "competing for women to taking care of their offspring."

This means that once a male genius nears forty and has children, his once-great mind loses its ability to do much of anything except argue with T-ball coaches and carp about the price of gasoline.

The report also found that marriage significantly dampens the male genius's desire for scientific achievement, perhaps because he must now accept the fact that he will occasionally be dispatched to the grocery store for diapers and tampons. It's a place where, his wife assures him, "nobody cares about your big ol' brain."

So he will wander the aisles, remembering past glories. And he'll be inexplicably drawn to the grape tomatoes.

21

Animal Instincts

Meet My New Rock Band—
The Cancer-Smelling Dogs!

When I sent my husband and daughter to "look at the cute kittens" at the pet store one Saturday morning, I have to admit it was just to get them out of the house so I could finally watch the finale of *For Love or Money 2*.

Thirty minutes later, my six-year-old was calling on the cell phone.

"Please, Mommy," she started slowly; then the rest came spilling out: "He's-so-cute-he-lets-me-hold-him-and-he-purrs-a-lot-and-I-wanna-name-him-Button."

Oh, for shit's sake. Good thing I hadn't sent them to the Lexus dealership or we'd be living off mayonnaise sandwiches. Again.

"Honey," I said, freeze-framing that little swamp slut Erin on the TV screen with my magic PAUSE button. "We already have two very old, mostly senile cats. It wouldn't be fair to them."

"Waaaaah! I don't see why we can't get just one little kitten! *You're mean!*"

I told my husband to put our daughter back on the phone.

"Oh, okay. Bring Button home, and we'll make it work." They gushed with gratitude and I hung up, wondering exactly what had just happened.

Thirty minutes later, Sophie raced in and shoved a shaking Button into my lap. For the first few days, things went great. Button was *no* trouble. In fact, he never, actually, moved. He lay in a tight ball, sleeping, while Sophie and her friends squealed at him to "get up and play!" It was like he was stuffed.

Finally, after he roused long enough to pee on my nightgown, I decided to take him to the vet.

"He's stressed," the vet said.

"*He's* stressed? What about me?" The two big fat liars who'd sworn they'd take care of him had barely been seen since.

As it turned out, Button was suffering from an intestinal ailment. For this, I had to push his little face back tight like Joan Rivers, pry his jaws open with my finger, and shove a pill down his throat.

"Wow, can you make him stop yelping like that?" Hubby asked. "I don't think he wants to take that pill."

Five spit-outs later, the pill was safely lodged in Button's tummy to work its wonders. The next day, he was much better; a week later, he was climbing up the draperies and pooping earnestly about the house in every possible location except the two litter boxes I'd bought for him.

Two more vet visits (I went to one with paw-print poop stains on my shirt, and *I didn't even care*) and Button was all better. I, however, wasn't sleeping well, because he'd taken to chewing on my toes all night long, forcing me to dream of tenement rats.

I thought that Button might finally earn his keep the day the lizard arrived.

I know that one of the worst things a parent can do is to pass silly phobias on to their children but, in the case of the lizard, I couldn't help myself. Lizards terrify me.

When Hubby got home from work, I was standing on the couch, calling to Button to come catch the lizard, but he was way too busy taking a dump on my dining room rug and could not be disturbed.

"What's up?" Hubby asked Soph, who was standing on the coffee table.

"Mommie saw a lizard in the living room," she explained calmly.

"A lizard? Inside the house? Are you sure?"

"Of course we're sure," I said. "Why else would I be standing on this couch?"

"That's no help," he said smugly. "They're excellent climbers."

"That's no help; they're excellent climbers," I mock mouthed him. *"Get a broom and find him!"*

Lizards severely creep me out. Once, I went to a little boy's birthday party, and his grandpa had two of them latched to his earlobes. The children loved Paw-Paw's cool party trick; I fainted.

So when our unwelcome visitor sashayed across the floor *like he owned the place,* I felt light-headed again. Thank goodness my neighbor heard my screams.

"It's just a little fella," she cooed, holding a Tupperware container open to catch him. He dodged to the left and scampered under the chair that I will never be able to sit in again.

"Get your cats in here," she advised cheerily on the way out, brushing aside my pleas to come live with her. "He won't last long when they find him!"

Clearly, she didn't understand that any instinct my cats ever had has been snuffed by three squares a day from our friends at 9Lives. Unless I could figure a way to lure the lizard into a can labeled "Now tender and meatier!" no help there.

A man doing yard work next door was summoned. I offered him all the money in the house—five dollars—to find and remove the lizard.

"He won't hurt you," the man said slowly, as though he

were talking to some sort of half-wit standing on a couch. "They are actually wonderful at eating flies and mosquitoes."

He tried for about fifteen minutes, but the lizard skittered all over the room, eventually returning to the chair that I will now have to burn.

"We have to sleep at a motel tonight," I told Hubby later. "Make the arrangements."

"Don't be silly. Did you know that the lizard's waste products actually inhibit the growth of certain household bacteria?"

Okay, it's official. Everybody is on the lizard's side. Somewhere, he was under a chair grinning from creepy non-ear to non-ear.

We never found the lizard, but I'm afraid it's only because he's hiding in my closet, changing his colors to match my clothes.

I suppose things could be worse than having your house taken over by a shit-slinging kitten and a maniacal lizard.

Near the top of a long list of things I'm grateful for is that, as far as I know, not a single one of my neighbors owns a pet tiger. Hey, it's not as far-fetched as you may think. I just read where there are between five thousand and seven thousand tigers living in private homes in this country. And I'm guessing that they pretty much hog the remote.

Even people who don't have yards are buying exotic wild animals as casually as a baggie full of goldfish from Wal-Mart.

Recently, I read about a guy in Florida who used to play

Tarzan in B movies and whose 750-pound tiger escaped from his home. Presumably watching him walk down the street were the actor's other pets: two lions, a leopard, and a cougar.

Steve Sipek had his own mini-jungle at his home near Palm Beach, perhaps in an attempt to relive his sort-of glory days as Tarzan. We can only hope that Tobey Maguire doesn't start trying to sling webs from his fingertips if his career falters. It's just so J. J. Walker sad when people confuse the characters they play with the people they are in real life. Think about it. No one really says "Dy-no-mite!" with any degree of enthusiasm anymore.

Of course, most of the owners of wild animals aren't aging movie stars but regular people like you and me except they've been sprinkled with what I like to call "the stupid dust."

What other explanation for a normal person to buy a wild animal? One story I read while doing a (very) little research on this subject suggested that owners of wildcats like that edge, or "spunk," of living with a wild animal. The "rush" of all this "spunk" was said to be "awesome." As I said, stupid dust. A woman in Washington State said her wildcat routinely runs off with her clothes whenever she gets dressed. Great. Now they're cross-dressing, too.

Sadly, like those pitiful dyed green and pink chicks that used to sit in dime store incubators like little punk rockers on a stage every Easter, cute doesn't last.

The experts are always warning these big-cat collectors that trouble can surface in the animal's adolescence when the formerly cuddlesome cub takes to growling, lunging, slamming doors, and sarcastically making little *L* shapes on its forehead every time you leave the room.

Well, almost.

As much as I adore my normal-size cats, you'd think that I might also enjoy the company of a dog, right? The truth is, I don't like 'em. Never have; never will. When you tell someone that you don't like dogs, they usually give you a look that falls somewhere in between pity and outright disgust.

They just don't get why I wouldn't want to be hanging around an animal that has been known to eat not only its own poo but the poo of others it finds in the yard.

This is not rocket science to me. It's a simple household rule: If you're a shit-eater, you're not living with me.

Naturally, since I don't like dogs, they sense this intuitively and totally respect my feelings. This respect is demonstrated by jumping on me, often knocking me to the ground, licking me, and doing unspeakable things while wrapped around my leg. The more I back away and mumble, "Nice doggie, now go play in the street," the more they seem to love me.

The only dog we ever had when I was growing up was a mutt who lived with us just long enough to rip everything on the clothesline to shreds and eat my favorite Davy Jones poster. I can still remember Davy's cute brown eyes dangling in a soggy mess from the corner of the beast's jaw.

The last time I saw Blackie (hey, nobody ever said we were particularly original dog owners), he was headed toward the woods behind our house wearing my training bra on his backside and chewing the remains of a mood ring.

That said, I accept that most dogs are plenty smart. I've always been impressed by how they can sniff drugs and even bombs using their keen sense of irony, I mean smell.

Unfortunately, I'm kind of freaked out about the newest revelation about dogs. There is indisputable scientific evidence that dogs can actually smell cancer on you. Now, I'm sure your first thought is the same as mine: *What a cool name for a rock band: Cancer-Smelling Dogs.*

After that thought passed, I realized that, because I am a profound hypochondriac, now I have to fret every time I visit my friend down the street and her enormous rug of a retriever lunges for me. Does Colby do this because he loves me or because he's trying to alert me to a life-threatening medical condition? Is he saying, as he slobbers onto my shirt and nuzzles my earlobes, "Timmy's trapped in the well, oh, no, what I meant to say is that you really should have that pancreas checked out." Well, is he?

Not long ago, I learned about a local service station that uses the services of an elderly hound to "sniff" tires. He can pinpoint a leak before you even know it's there. Amazing!

I hate to admit this, but it's obvious: Dogs have it all over my beloved but totally useless housecats.

I could drive up to the house on four flat tires, with a ticking bomb and a kilo of cocaine in the trunk, tumors hanging off me as big as pie plates, and my selfish cats would just yawn, stretch, and go back to sleep.

In the case of a woman with skin cancer, the dog not only detected the problem but set about trying to remove it himself! That's cool, although it's going to be a billing nightmare for her HMO. I can picture the back-of-the-phone-book ads: The doctor is *in* and it's Rin Tin Tin!

22

What Women Want

If You Can't Be Imprisoned for Life, Could You Maybe Act Just a Little Gay?

Suddenly, being a housewife is downright trendy. In two of this season's biggest TV hits, housewives are either "desperate" or "swapped." My, oh, my, what a refreshing change from the days when a housewife's only virtue was that she might "have the magic of Clorox 2."

Finally, housewives are hot—whether they're living lives of loud desperation on Wisteria Lane as in ABC's megahit *Desperate Housewives* or they're raising fat, pampered brats over on *Wife Swap*.

Long ignored by everyone except peanut butter manufacturers, housewives are finally getting some ink for being sexy, complicated creatures that are too often underestimated. In other words, we're here, we leer, get used to it.

Having dinner with my stay-at-home mom friends the

other night, we had to wonder why we don't look like the babes on *Desperate Housewives*. I feel a little like most of New York City's female population must've felt while watching *Sex and the City* for the first time. Who were these gorgeous women wearing five-hundred-dollar Manolos and little else as they bedded most of Manhattan? Doesn't anybody have to get up in the morning?

To be fair, there is one harried *Desperate* housewife who is raising the World's Worst Little Boys. Even wearing jam, though, she's still beautiful and loves to show off those chiseled work-out arms that I've grown to hate in other women. Whither the batwings that we get from having too little time to work out and too much time to finish little Sally's *Shark Tale* Happy Meal?

I take *Desperate Housewives* for what it is: a fun, fluffy farce with a slight *Twin Peaks* edge to it. Still, I feel insecure when I compare my housewifely look to theirs. Around the house, I wear a Kathie Lee floral shift that has seen better days. It's fabulously comfortable and ideal for vacuuming. But it's nothing like the put-together look modeled by Marcia Cross of *DH* as she toothbrush-scrubs her toilet while wearing a scarf tied jauntily around her graceful neck.

On the surprisingly poignant reality show *Wife Swap*, we see women more like ourselves: a little chubby, a little loud, a lot loving.

The great thing about *Wife Swap* (settle down, right-wingers; there's no hanky panky among spouses here) is that there's no hero or villain. Granola mom and SUV mom are right some of the time. And mercifully neither one believes that a bottle of bleach contains anything approaching magic.

But both shows do illustrate, in an over-the-top way, that American women are getting a little screwy when it comes to picking our mates. And increasingly, mind-bendingly desperate.

How else do you explain the hundreds of sacks of love letters that show up at Scott Peterson's San Quentin cell every week?

Murder conviction? Oh, nobody's perfect. To these women, Peterson is just as cute as a bug's ear. They apparently assume that if you're good-looking and famous, even if it's for murdering your wife and kid, then you'd be a great catch.

But you never see men doing this, hons. You never hear about men writing Andrea Yates or Susan Smith in prison, do you?

That's because men are statistically more likely to read about heinous family-killing crimes committed by a woman and say, "Damn, that bitch is crazy!"

A California criminal justice professor who was asked to explain the mail-to-murderers phenomenon said it usually happens when women don't believe the accused is guilty and they want to come to the rescue of someone whom the whole world is against, someone who is "beleaguered."

For my money, beleaguered beats dead any day.

Yep, Scott Peterson is a prize catch, all right. And now, he's single!

O. J. Simpson, who has finally suspended his exhaustive personal crusade to find "the real killer" of his wife on finer public golf courses throughout the state of Florida, never has a problem finding willing and wonderfully attractive women to date.

What up?

Not only do we "desperate" women want to date murderers, but we also want to date gay men.

Why else would we invite *Queer Eye for the Straight Guy*'s Fab Five into our homes to "make over" our husbands? I know I'd like to.

Why can't our straight-guy husbands understand that we're sick of fighting about where to hang the velour rug depicting the poker-playing dogs? I want to drape it lovingly over the top of the garbage can on Monday morning just before the truck comes rumbling down the alley. He wants to hang it over the buffet like it's some kind of rare tapestry from the Moron Dynasty.

While I don't want to correspond with murderers just because they would never leave their undershorts on the floor, I also don't want to be married to a gay man. I couldn't take the fault-finding.

It would take a nanosecond for *Queer Eye*'s menswear counselor Carson to dis my husband's "Got Duckheads?"

approach to fashion, but I wouldn't have time to feel superior once Thom, the decorator, spotted our ironing board
as nightstand. Culinary expert Ted would sniff and make
gagging noises over our grocery-store wine. And, sure,
grooming guru Kyan would lecture my husband about
proper shaving ("It's not a race, bro!"), but we'd both suffer when culture expert Jai examined our pitiful collection
of CDs. ("The Eagles? *The Eagles!* Get this couple some Be-
yoncé, *stat!*")

Every woman I know is gaga about these five gay men
who "makeover" the looks, and the lair, of a particularly
needy straight guy. In the end, the gays got the girls. It's
high school all over again, but look who's kicking butt!
Sure, Bubba may have snickered at the sensitive young man
who sewed sequins on his cousin's wedding gown back in
the day, but who's laughing now? I can't *hear* you!

The beauty of *Queer Eye* is its ability to reduce a huge,
hulking straight construction worker into the kind of guy
who waxes his back hair, quotes John Donne, and literally
weeps with gratitude for a makeover, hugging his five new
friends until they have to pull away.

When the Fab Five's work is complete, straight guy usually turns, teary-eyed, to survey his redecorated crib, transformed from messy, dorm-room mishmash to a sleek yet
warm tribute to the wonders wrought by Thom let loose
with the Bravo credit card in Pottery Barn, Urban Outfit-
ters, and Pier 1.

Although ratings are huge among the straight set, some members of the gay community have protested the show's "perpetuation of gay stereotypes." As one gay activist told public radio recently, "Gay men can dress sloppy, waste a weekend watching sports on TV, and not know how to cook, too."

Note to gay activist: These are not good things. Learn how to take a compliment, would you?

They say that the show's flamboyant gay stars make it seem as though every gay man is a boa-wearing oversexed weirdo.

I don't get that. With the exception of the always-randy Carson, whose wit is eat-your-young mean, the rest just seem like very smart, very kind guys who just want to help a unibrowed brother out.

In the words of Rodney King, can't we all just go to the spa, slap on some eucalyptus exfoliating cream, and learn how to shave with something besides a Bic disposable? I thought so.

23

Bush on Marriage

"Bin Laden, Bin Schmaden! 50 Cent and Vivica Fox Are in Crisis!"

I received one of those Mr. Wonderful dolls as a gag gift for Valentine's Day. If you haven't seen one yet, allow me to explain. Mr. Wonderful is small enough to fit on a key chain and depicts a square-jawed neatly dressed man who, when pressed in the tummy, says some pretty hilarious things. Things like, "Let's just cuddle" or "You've worked hard today—let me cook dinner tonight" or "Awwww, can't your mother stay at least one more week?"

While I'm quite taken with Mr. Wonderful (who can resist a soothing male voice saying, "Here, you take the remote. As long as I'm with you, I don't care what we watch"?), it occurred to me that men have every right to expect a Mrs. Wonderful to be in production, too.

I mean it's not as if we women are perfect. Well, at least

most of y'all aren't. So I've come up with my own list of Mrs. Wonderful's possible utterances. Feel free to think up some of your own.

Things a "Mrs. Wonderful" Might Say

"What? There's a new episode of *Grey's Anatomy* on tonight? Oh, let's watch that some other time. I'd much rather make love."

"You know, I really like the speed limit you have chosen and I wouldn't dream of telling you the best way to get to Chip and Susie's house. I'll just sit here and be a thoughtful, considerate passenger."

"Oh, honey, do you really think your mom would give me some pointers in the kitchen? I would love to be able to cook for you and serve you just the way she did! Oh, and shouldn't we be making love right about now, mister?"

"*SportsCenter* is on again? Why it seems as if it comes on every hour on the hour. Aren't we lucky to live in a country like this? ESPN truly separates us from the savages!"

"Sweetheart, do you think you could wear that old Carolina sweatshirt with the tung oil stains and the holes in it to have dinner with my family just one more time? We all just *love* you in it!"

"Now, honey pie, you don't need to know where the car keys or the milk and bread are. That's what you have me for!"

"Oh, fudge! You forgot our anniversary again? Well,

heh-heh, I know something we could do to celebrate that wouldn't cost a thing!"

Marriage would be easy if we all acted more like our key chains, wouldn't it?

With the U.S. divorce rate at 57 percent, you have to wonder why President George Bush has decided to spend $1.5 billion of your tax dollars to develop programs that will encourage people to get married instead of just live together.

Bush's "healthy marriage initiative" calls for gobs of federally funded counseling on the benefits of marriage through mentoring and instruction in how to make a marriage work. (Short version: "Just let her win.")

The notion of the government getting into the business of matchmaking is a hoot. What next? TV spots with Dick Cheney as a caftan-wearing marriage voodoo priestess? Condoleeeeeza offering tips for the lovelorn via those eight-bucks-a-minute "love hotlines"?

Making healthy marriages is a laudable goal, but it's a notion that needs a high-profile test case like, say, Britney Spears and Jason Allen Alexander, a prime example of a couple who never gave their marriage a fair chance. Under the Bush plan, there would never have been any time for Kevin Federline.

Under the Bush plan, Britney and Jason would have been given orders to work on their fifty-five-hour marriage and iron out their differences. (He thought "gravy train with old high school buddy"; she thought "Face it, after five sour appletinis I'd pretty much marry Christina Aguilera, who is hairier, by the way.")

In Bush's world, Brit and Jason wouldn't just be able to go before a judge and whine for a quickie annulment.

No, no. It happened too fast. What God and a half-dozen really wasted witnesses hath put together, let no judge put asunder in just a few minutes. Under the Bush plan, a federal bureaucrat could have been dispatched to the scene of the breakup and convinced the couple that it was purely possible for Britney, one of the richest and most popular entertainers in the world, to give it all up in order to settle down and make fat Louisiana babies with a, uh, college student.

Can we be far removed from a divorce requiring an official letter from the President of the United States to be final?

We get it. Marriage should not be entered into lightly. But Bush should know that most couples already get premarital counseling for free from their minister. Admittedly, in Las Vegas, this is probably reduced to an Elvis impersonator advising the couple, "Don't be cruel." Then again, what more is there to say, really?

The president's weird marriage-or-bust program could also have helped those headline-grabbing former shackmates

Ben Affleck and Jennifer Lopez. If only they could have had a sit-down with the leader of the free world before deciding to split. J. Lo could've expressed her frustration with Ben's gambling and womanizing, and Ben could've said, "Look, we all know that I'll never be truly happy with anyone except Matt Damon, so let's just stop pretending."

Y'all know I'm right.

I worry about Bush's "save the marriage at all costs" mentality. One couple I'd like to nudge into divorce court would be Mr. and Mrs. Kobe Bryant.

I have to admit it: I was on Kobe Bryant's side till he bought his wife an eight-carat purple diamond that cost more than four million bucks to atone for that pesky rape charge. Hallmark, which has a card for almost everything, must not have had one in the "Sorry I Strayed, But It Was Consensual" category.

On the other hand—yep, the one that sports my modest three-quarter carat diamond ring bought from a pawnshop, no less—maybe Kobe's wife had the right idea.

Next time Hubby forgets to take out the garbage? Let's seeee, that's one pair of sapphire earrings. If he eats the last Eskimo Pie (again), that's one tennis bracelet on the Kobe Scale of Remorse.

My heart goes out to Kobe's wife, with her sad Precious Moments doll eyes. As I watched her stroke his hands during the World's Most Humiliating Press Conference when the news first broke, I had to wonder how she could sit there while he described her as his "backbone," "soul mate," and similar gibberish.

She did "her duty" on live TV. But sister-hon should have accepted that ring only long enough to hold it under Kobe's nose and say something on the order of, "Fool, you need to put that hunka junk where the sun don't shine."

While I don't think it's smart to force people into marriage through a guvmint program, I'm actually a big fan of weddings—old-fashioned ones, that is. That's why I'm so distressed to see the disturbing trend of tacky engagement announcements. You know the ones I'm talking about. The bridal page picture where He is tightly wrapped around Her in their best impersonation of a couple desperately in need of a room.

Now I realize that we live in an age in which most people actually believe you can—heck, you *should*—meet your soul mate on a TV show catfight filmed in a borreyed castle somewhere. Therefore, maybe we've let a lot of wedding customs go by the wayside.

Still, I must speak out against the "modern" engagement photos of couples wearing bathing suits or tube tops and muscle shirts looking slightly hungover. And, at the risk of offending more than a few friends and relatives, I don't think grooms belong in engagement photos at all.

One reason is they're impossible to pose. How many

times have you seen the studio portrait where she is standing behind her beloved, arms wrapped around him like a sumo chokehold? They sure look happy.

Call me old school, but I think engagement portraits should be of the bride only. Men have no business being in the picture. Just show up at the chapel and remember not to smash cake in her face on the big day. You're a guy, for heaven's sake. No one cares what you look like, and neither should you.

The tacky wedding write-up is another pet peeve. There is simply no need to advise us, as one wedding announcement did recently, that "two have become one during a spectacular Maui honeymoon trip."

Oh, precious Lord.

Ditto the fact that your children served as your junior attendants. We know you've shacked since Clinton's first term; just don't rub our noses in it.

As a native Southerner, it's possible that I am irrationally traditional on such matters. We Southerners cling like kudzu to our traditions. Every so often, though, things go awry. I'm remembering a bridal shower I helped host in which a friend thought it would be a good idea to have tiny plastic cherubs frozen in the punch bowl ice ring. Instead of evoking the image of merry cupids that we had hoped for, more than a half dozen guests gasped in horror and demanded to know, "Why are there dead babies floating in the punch?"

Like picking a wedding photographer based solely on which one of your redneck cousins has the biggest lens and best chance of staying sober, the floating cupids seemed like a good idea at the time.

And speaking of wedding photography, y'all show some love to Catherine Zeta-Jones, who has gone to court, repeatedly, to claim that her wedding day was ruined by unauthorized photographers.

Oh, how I have cried myself to sleep thinking about how CZJ has had to suffer. And Michael Douglas, too. They're outraged that the paparazzi snapped unauthorized pictures of their wedding at the Plaza Hotel years ago.

My heartless friend Susan thinks it's ridiculous. "I mean," says Susan, "doesn't this woman know there are people with real problems out here in the real world?"

What can I tell you? Susan clearly can't comprehend deep pain. After all, as I pointed out, CZJ said that both she and Michael broke down and cried in phone calls to friends about how tacky tabloid photos ruined their most special day. At least the most special since Michael's last wedding.

One gets the impression that Michael Douglas would say just about anything to keep the missus happy, and for that he gets major props. But it does tarnish his macho image a bit to see him wringing his hands in public about how "devastated" and "emotional" he is about photos that "made the reception look like a disco."

The Zeta-Jones–Douglases did allow that the pain and

stress of the wedding day ordeal, while irreparable, could be mollified somewhat by $800,000.

Big of them.

To the two of them I'd say, that having a wedding at the Plaza Hotel doesn't entitle you to a lot of privacy. Hell, even I have had tea at the Plaza and roamed its hallways, so that should tell you those folks are about as discriminating as a pre-Trimspa Anna Nicole Smith at an all-you-can-eat chitlins buffet.

Marriage isn't easy, even with federal grants and lawsuits to help. Perhaps the Zeta-Jones–Douglases can bravely soldier on, despite this numbing tragedy of disco receptions and allegations of matching chicken necks on bride and groom. Perhaps some of Bush's counseling could help them work through the stages of grief: denial, anger, greed, and a new house in Bermuda.

Works for me.

PART V

Southern-Style Silliness

24

Illness and Death, Southern Style

(Or Why I Will Never Eat London Broil Again)

I've always been an obituary junkie. If there's a long, fabulous obit accompanied by a picture obviously taken at least forty years earlier while wearing a sailor hat, then I'm hooked. If there's a nickname in quotes, say, Red Eye, Tip Top, or simply, Zeke, then my entire day is made.

I don't like obituaries that don't list the cause of death. Even if the newly dead was ninety-six, one can't assume. I crave details. I must know whether death resulted from accident, disease, or simply an unfortunate tuna casserole.

I don't like obituaries that don't list charities. Not long ago, I read about a Wisconsin mother of six who died at seventy-one and specified that, in lieu of flowers, donations be made to any organization supporting the impeachment of President Bush. You just know she died with her little fists all curled up, mad as a mule chewing bumblebees.

I don't like obituaries that just list the bare facts: name, age, place of death, relatives, funeral details. No, no. I want to know that the deceased loved the Atlanta Braves, Reese's Pieces, Dale Jr., and going to Mr. Tang's Imperial Wok on all-you-can-eat crab legs night. People, is this too much to ask?

Occasionally, readers are rewarded with a list of survivors that includes beloved family pets: "Joe is also survived by his faithful standard poodle, Rhett, and a somewhat sickly betta fish he purchased at Wal-Mart only a week before he died and had named Stumpy for reasons unknown to anyone else."

I like obituaries that aren't afraid to let loose a little bit. "Crossing Jordan," "racing into the arms of the Almighty," and "leaving all earthly cares behind" (including, perhaps, an unpaid Belk charge card and that nagging thumpa-lumpa-lump noise that had been coming from beneath the hood of the LeSabre for a couple of months now) are powerful descriptions, all.

I love obituaries that take the time to point out that the deceased died "peacefully, surrounded by his entire family." Celebrities appear to be especially good at this. Not only are they rich and famous, but their families can assemble dutifully and peacefully from around the globe on a moment's notice. I hate them.

Still, it's a tremendous accomplishment for any family to be assembled in one room *and* peaceful! But, unlike the Thanksgiving table, in which all manner of grievances tend to spill out over the creamed onions, deathbed etiquette demands that Aunt Pearl refrain from calling Uncle Gene "that lying apostate of hell who cheated on me back in '57."

I'm too young to be talking about death and dying, I guess, but it's a Southern thing to obsess over these matters. Funeralizing is second only to hospital visitation in occasions that call for you to dress in your best Jaclyn Smith for Kmart Collection.

I did an inordinate amount of hospital-visiting when my friend Lula was admitted.

The best part of our visits was listening to this wiry little redneck woman who was her roommate on the other side of the curtain.

Here's something you need to know: Little old Southern redneck women are always pissed off. They can't help "theyselves." Maybe it's from a lifetime of living with a man who thinks a talking bass plaque is a suitable fortieth anniversary gift.

Lula's roommate was one of the most hardcore little old rednecks I've ever encountered, so naturally I just pulled up a chair and listened while Lula just scowled.

Azelene had started firing questions as soon as Lula got settled into her bed.

"What're *you* in for?" she snapped.

"Oh," said Lula, "we thought it was my heart, but it turned out to be my gall bladder, so I'm going to be just fine."

"Hmmmph!" Azelene snorted. "Don't you let 'em tell you you didn't have no heart attack, honey. When I had my first heart attack, they tried to tell me it was just indigestion. They don't know *nothing!* Damn thing like t' have blowed the whole back of my heart off!"

Lula gasped.

"That was almost as bad as the time I had to call 911 on account of my backbone was a-poking outside of my skin. They said it wasn't, but they don't know pea turkey squat. You don't believe me? Just feel this scar on my back ratch 'ere. Go on! Feel of it, honey. You know, I've lost all the feeling in all my arms and laigs ever since I got the sugar."

Redneck vocabulary tip: A good Southern redneck doesn't know from diabetes. It's always *the sugar.* They also call Alzheimer's *old-timer's* and don't know that's funny. (In a related vocabulary note, redneck old people always call SUVs *SOBs,* and they really don't know what they're saying. You haven't lived until you've heard old Aunt Bettisue say, quite innocently, "That there SOB's gonna run right over us, he's so big.")

Redneck Southern women of all ages love to dress up any ailment, no matter how minor. My redneck friend Verna-Lynn is particularly blessed with a colorful vocabulary when it comes to her "ladies' time."

"I swear I'm flushing clots the size of a London broil," she announced one day over lunch.

Check, please.

Elderly redneck women will go to dramatic lengths to get attention. My friend's mama used to look both ways down the street before carefully lying down in the shrubbery near her front door with just her legs showing from the kneecaps down.

The first time I saw this, it was naturally quite upsetting, and I raced to help. My friend stopped me. "Oh, hell, hon, that's just Mama's way of getting attention. She's forever hiding in the shrubbery and pretending to have blacked out. Come on in and borrow that casserole dish you needed; she'll crawl out directly."

I tell you this so you'll have a bit of context when you consider Azelene's conversations.

During a break in a long discussion about her latest bout of hemorrhoids ("I swanee they're as big as sofa cushions"), I noticed a spit cup surface from under Azelene's bedcovers.

For a few moments, all you could hear in the hospital room was the sound of an old woman's spit hitting the side of a Tar Heels 1993 National Champions mug. The relative peace was disrupted, as it always is when the Southern Redneck Woman has company in the hospital.

A friend had dropped by to visit but confessed he was nervous. "I haven't been in a hospital since my brother shot hisself in the leg on account of trying to commit Hare Krishna."

Somebody brought fried chicken.

Lula and I, bored by the *Falcon Crest* reunion that was taking place on the TV overhead, just soaked it all up, including a lengthy visit from Azelene's preacher, a thunder-voiced Pentecostal who sold double-wides by day. He'd come straight from his weekly visit counseling all the lost sheep in the "pentenchurary."

"Did you see my Edwin?" Azelene asked.

"Shore did. He said he didn't rob that Kangaroo Mart, and he can prove it."

"Course he can! My baby's innocent as the day he was born. Which like t've killed me. He weighed damn near sixteen pounds, you know. They had to remove all my internal organs just to prize him out. They say you can't live without a liver, but I been doin' just fine. I knew they didn't put everything back. Saw it sittin' on the counter just like it needed some fried onions with it."

"Merciful heavens," Lula half groaned.

The next day, rolling out of Azelene's life forever, Lula waved good-bye. Azelene, not a sentimental sort, just yawned. "On your way out, tell that bony little hank o' hair out at the desk I need a pan. Did I tell you about my hemorrhoids?"

25

Want to "Talk Southern"?

Here's Some Advice from My Abode to Yours

I had to call the phone company after a small hurricane passed through, ripped the line down, and left it in a mangled mess on my deck.

This didn't go well. See, I live in North Carolina, and the phone company representative—who for some inane reason began every sentence with "Now, Miss Riventybarky, we understand that you are frustrated" while simultaneously adding to my frustration—was elsewhere, like Bangalore.

Not that there's anything wrong with that. Some of my best friends are Bangaloreans. Okay, not really. I'm from the South, where when we say, "The phone line's down, and y'all need to get a truck over here to put it back up," this is somehow greeted by the Bangalorean as completely unreliable.

"Miss Riventybarky," she began, "have you considered that perhaps the phone is unplugged or there is a problem with the, uh, [sound of shuffling translation guides] jack inside the [shuffling again] abode?"

I distinctly remember grabbing an unopened bottle of wine at this point and considering banging it open on the side of the kitchen counter, thus bypassing the more time-consuming corkscrew method.

"I don't live in an abode; I live in a house, a house without any telephone service and my name is *not* Riventybarky!"

"Miss Riventybarky, now I do understand that you are frustrated—"

"Arrrgggh!"

Long story short, I finally convinced my almond-eyed friend on the far side of the world that I really did have enough sense to recognize a tattered phone line on the ground. She finally agreed to believe me, and we all gave peace a chance. The very next morning, a fabulous crew from the local phone company showed up in whipping rains and "got 'er done."

I was thinking about this because I just learned that my Southern hometown is now a major "call center" for Verizon, a telecommunications giant whose name comes from the Latin *Veri,* which means "bladder" and *zon,* which means "elongated." I don't care; it still sounds cool.

Anywho, the funny part is that here we are, in the Deep South, and we're the call center servicing, get this, Metropolitan New York City! What elongated bladder genius thought this would be a good match?

NY CALLER: My phone's broken and you need to fix it today.

US: Todaaaay? Do what?

NY CALLER: Yes, today, Gomer. I'm a very busy and important person wearing way too much hair product.

US: I understand your, uh, frustration—

NY CALLER: "I'll give you somethin' to be frustrated about. Now get the grits outta your mouth and fix my f-ing phone."

US: I bet you wouldn't talk like that in front of your mama. *Click.*

Thing is, we don't talk like the rest of the country, and we're frankly relieved.

Remember this above all else: Southerners despise bad news and loathe sharing it without some gloss. We invented that classic joke about the beloved cat that was killed while his owner was away from home. It's the one where the neighbor bluntly says "Your cat's dead," and his devastated friend says, "Couldn't you tell me nicer? Ease me into it? Tell me the cat got up on the roof and then tumbled down and died instantly and without any undue suffering?" A few weeks later, the same neighbor is forced to relay some sad news again. Remembering his friend's request, he begins, "See, your grandma was on the roof. . . ."

This near-pathological avoidance of bad news has led to such famous Southernisms as using "the late unpleasantness" to describe the War Between the States. We don't just come right out and say something; we have to cozy up to it like the cat to the cream jar.

One of the best examples of classic Southern understatement is found in the word *unfortunate,* which, in the South, can describe anything from losing all one's earthly possessions in a house fire ("Selma and Jim-Bob experienced a most unfortunate fire") to describing your exceedingly homely girl-cousin as having "a most unfortunate nose."

Unfortunate, you'll notice, is usually paired with *most* for purposes of emphasis. Don't use *very,* or you will be revealed to be the outsider that you truly are and told to go back to sprinkling sugar on your grits and similar abominations.

Here's a quick checklist for dos and don'ts down South. No thanks are necessary; it's thanks enough that I am able to help.

DON'T say *yous.* Practice saying *y'all, y'all's,* or *yalls'es* without sneering. Get over yourself.

DON'T discuss how much money you make or how much you paid for your leaf blower, standing mixer, lawn tractor, shoes, and so on. Southerners don't do that, because it's tacky.

DO realize that tacky is the worst label that can be applied to any person, behavior, or event in the South. As in, "Mama said Raylene's bridal shower coming three months after she had the baby was as tacky as those Sam's Club mints she served right out of the carton."

DON'T criticize our driving. We know where the turn lane is and what it's for. We're just messing with you.

DON'T accuse us of being "thin-skinned" or lacking a sense of humor. We laugh plenty behind your back.

DO remember that *barbecue* is a noun, never a verb, and it's a holy noun at that.

DON'T question the superiority of Atlantic Coast Conference basketball. This could lead to a most unfortunate coma.

Of course, as is often the case, we in the South can be our own worst enemy. I recently learned that there is a course being taught at the University of South Carolina that helps Southerners lose their accents. Can you believe it?

My ox is gored, my tater fried, and, yes, the red has indeed been licked off my candy.

You see, I have a dog in this fight. The notion that you should try to get rid of your Southernisms makes me madder'n a wet setting hen.

The professor, Erica Tobolski, says that she is teaching her students how to stop talking Southern and start using Standard American Dialect (or, appropriately, SAD for short). This way, we can all sound exactly alike. Isn't that just gooder'n grits and finer'n frog's hair?

Of course it's not. The truth is, I wouldn't give Ms. Tobolski air if 'n she was trapped in a jug. Which it sounds to me like she may have been. For some time. How else do you explain such oxygen-deprived plumb foolishness? I swear if that woman's brains were dynamite, an explosion wouldn't even ruffle her hair on a windy day.

"Many students come to see me because they want to sound less country," Ms. Tobolski told the Associated Press. They want to be able to turn their native Southern accent on and off so it doesn't embarrass them when they travel or go on job interviews.

Y'all want to know what embarrasses me? That any right-thinking daughter or son of Dixie would sign up for this insulting course. Do we really want to sound like the "You've got mail" guy or the android who tells us to "Press One for Customer Service"?

Answer me. *Do we?*

Oh, "hail" no.

I have a friend who travels to the Northeast a lot on business. She's a high-powered, successful executive, and she takes pride in her Southern accent.

Going toe-to-toe with Boston lawyers on their turf, she refers to them as *y'all,* but they have learned that to question her brainpower would just prove that they're the ones dumber'n a sack of hammers.

What we need to do is celebrate our accent and nevah, evah try to change it. If we try to get rid of it so others will think better of us, we will have lost our Southern soul, trading the essence of ourselves for what?

So take that course, if you must. But don't be surprised if you end up spending your empty little life stumbling around just as lost and prone to misery as a blind horse in a punkin patch.

Y'all know I'm right.

26

Flu Strikes at Christmas

(And Nobody Had a Silent Night)

If you're going to go and get yourself a really noisy, nasty intestinal virus, it's always best to do it while visiting your in-laws for the holidays. That way, the entire extended family, which is staying overnight in the small brick ranch house that your husband grew up in, can be treated to a cacophony of sounds that they will long remember.

And that way, one by one, they can step, in their bathrobes, to the closed door of the one full bath in the house and shout, with a mixture of pity and fear, "You doing all right in there?"

To which you scream a loving *"Go away!"*

Maybe I'll write about my Christmas night "song" one day in one of those tiny little volumes with treacly prose that sells so well during December. As I snuggled into my husband's boyhood bed mere hours before the attack on my innards was launched, I read five of these little books, all filled with misty-eyed memories of hearth and home and angels and snowmen. None offered a memory like the one I was about to generate for all the family to snicker about for years to come.

Hours later, my humiliation complete, I lay in bed and tried to ignore the smell of frying country ham. A brother-in-law timidly offered to bring me some breakfast, but I told him to just bypass the middleman and throw it directly into the toilet on my behalf. All morning long, I could over-hear the conversation between niece and nephew, aunt and uncle and so forth.

"I heard her at about four thirty," said one.

"Naw, it was closer to two thirty. You must've slept through the first round."

Oh, sweet Jesus, make them stop.

It didn't take a genius to figure out that this was going to permanently scar the younger members of the family who, mere hours before, had happily been playing with a whoopee cushion brought by Santa himself. Now the sound wasn't all that funny.

"Do you think she's gonna die?" I heard one ask.

"Sure sounds like it," another said solemnly.

A relative in Texas called with holiday greetings, and I heard my husband cheerfully announce that I couldn't come to the phone because "She's busy at both ends!" Great. There's one less state I can show my face in again.

The rest of the morning, I heard the relatives leave, cheerfully reminding my mother-in-law to "Lysol the doorknobs!" My husband's family believes that Lysol solves everything. I was deathly afraid they might sneak in and try to spray me from top to bottom while I slept. And dreamed of writing "Upheaval at the In-Laws': A Christmas Song."

Yeah, that'll sell.

I'm not sure a flu shot would've helped in my case, but I couldn't get one anyway, because I was too young. I told everybody that and enjoyed it mightily. It's the most fun I've had since I told the nurse running the church Bloodmobile that "I can't donate on account of I don't weigh enough."

Oh, settle down. I've signed away my organs and, frankly, the way that guy at the Optimist Club booth stared at me when I was signing away my dead corneas, I was a little scared he was going to take 'em right then.

But give blood? Uh, not so much. So instead of being the weenie that I am, fainting in front of an entire basement full of people, I said I didn't weigh enough.

Because this is the South, where people are civilized to your face, there were no follow-up questions such as, "Honey, your ass appears to need its own area code, so I'm guessing you do weigh more than ninety-five pounds."

She sure was thinking it, though.

When I took my octogenerian dad to the drugstore to get his flu shot, I couldn't believe the crowd. The line snaked through eight—count 'em, eight—aisles. For the first hour, it barely moved. When we finally saw one man walk by, pointing to his arm and then making a *V* for victory sign, we burst into spontaneous applause.

The funny thing about getting in line for a flu shot is that, if you are not of a certain age, you get dirty looks. I was just there for moral support, but I could see the raised eyebrows: *Hmmm, she better be missing some kidneys or something.*

I recognize the look because it's the same one I use when I see someone park in a handicapped space and then cheerily skip into the mall having figured out that sometimes it's cool to borrow Great-gran's Taurus.

"It's not for me," I stammered. "I'm just here with my dad. I don't want a flu shot. In fact, I wish I could give back the one I got seven years ago so that others might be helped."

Ahhh. Their faces relaxed, and they put down their torches. I had been afraid that I was one step away from the old "witch test," where they would dunk me in a vat of NyQuil to see if I would sink.

When you're in a drugstore for that long, you gotta read something, so I selected Dr. Phil's weight-loss cookbook. It wasn't a great choice, because it's so big and heavy that I had to pretty much kick it ahead on the floor with my foot like luggage while reading it. Dr. Phil's diet consists of meals like *Lunch:* Grilled salmon, steamed asparagus and leeks, and sweet potato soufflé. *Dinner:* Roasted chicken, steamed vegetable medley, and fat-free polenta cakes.

Yeah. Let me just call my personal chef and have her whip that shit up. Is Dr. Phil *on the pipe?*

Frankly, after a few hours in the flu line, I was convinced that what we'd have for supper that night would be stackable Lay's, Altoids, and some stationery with kittens on it. Yum!

This past winter, there was such a flu-shot frenzy that I wondered why there wasn't a Flu Channel. ("All Flu, All the Time!") complete with Weather Channel studs wearing yellow slickers and reporting live from the scene of Joe and Joan's four-poster mahogany bed. I can just see 'em clinging to the bedposts as they battle gale-force sneezes and wet hacking coughs while assuring us that "There's . . . not . . . much . . . time!"

It seems a cruel irony that flu season coincides with the busiest shopping season. At the mall, I desperately want to wear a surgical mask and gloves but I'm too chicken, fearful that shoppers will mistake me for Michael Jackson, who has been notoriously germ-phobic since he was just a small nut job growing up in Encino.

Post-flu, there are three types of antibacterial lotions in my purse these days and, like the in-laws, I've taken to spraying doorknobs with Lysol, sometimes while my guests are still touching them.

Even if I'd had a flu shot, there's no guarantee it would have been the right one. At least that's what everybody at the CDC (the Cootie Detection Center) down in Atlanta says. That's because every year there is a "new strain" of flu out there, mostly representing ominous sounding parts of the world like the Haiku Province, the Kung Pow Shrimp, and the Moo Goo Gai Pain. You never know which one's going to strike.

So somebody at the drug company has an office pool or a lucky dartboard and finally picks one and bazillions of Moo Goo vaccines are shipped out. But just when you start to relax, you discover that, as it turns out, that guess was completely wrong. That this year's flu strain was more of a Knockwurst–Type A, and epidemiologists around the world were left with egg foo yong on their faces.

I'd like to talk more about this, but I have to boil my mail. You just can't be too careful, hons.

27

Knitting, Boy Dinosaurs, and Chipotle

What Is a Category You Will Never See on *Jeopardy!*

Get this. Knitting is hip. In fact, knitting is almost as hip as chipotle these days. Women are forming "stitch 'n' bitch" clubs where they sit around and knit. This sounds like a giant step backwards to me. What's next? Getting together to make our own spray starch?

Knitting. You've got to be kidding. Before I hear from all the rabid pro-knitting nuts (oops, too late—more on that in a minute), let me say that I actually know a little something about knitting. I used to knit little purses for my friends in junior high, but then I *got a life.*

And about chipotle. Don't get me started. Nobody even knows how to pronounce this stuff, and now every restaurant you go to wants to put chipotle all over everything.

It reminds me of the old Monty Python skit where the

diner asks his waiter about the dessert specials, which turn out to be "rat pudding, rat pie, and strawberry tart." The customer looks perplexed. "Strawberry tart?" "Well," says the server, a tad apologetically, "there's *some* rat in it." Same with chipotle. I don't even know what it is, but it's on everything. Chipotle sauce, chipotle butter, chipotle beer. What next? "New, improved Hamburger Helper: Now with 50 percent more chipotle!"

Anyway, I was sitting around not knitting or eating chipotle the other night when I stumbled across a fascinating article about dinosaurs. See, it turns out that the real reason dinosaurs died out sixty-five million years ago was because a series of asteroid hits caused the skies to go dark and the Earth to grow cold.

This had a more serious effect than just making the dinosaurs hang out in the garages of their friends trying to get some cheap spray-tanning.

No, no. The real problem was that, as it turns out, boy dinosaurs are born more often when temperatures drop. After a while, there was little suspense in the dinosaur waiting room. It was, always, a boy.

And he was eating chipotle. No, no, just kidding.

For a while, I imagine this was a lot of fun. Dinosaurs all over the earth got to put their hooves up on the coffee table without being yelled at and could sit around with their buddies without being nagged to mow the rocks or whatever.

While I'm sure this was cause for great prehistoric merry-making, after a while, the old men's club just got kind of dull. All they ever did was hang out, eat way too many leaves, and just, generally, discuss Republican politics.

So, now you know how dinosaurs disappeared. Let's just hope that knitting and chipotle won't be far behind.

Okay, maybe just chipotle.

Knitters, I have discovered, don't have much of a sense of humor. Every time I crack on the knitters, I get irate letters. Who knew?

Judging from the, uh, passion, with which these people write letters, I have to say that it would not surprise me in the least to find a large hand-knit horse's head on the foot of my bed one day. Here was a typical letter from a woman I will simply call "Purl."

"Who do you think you are to put down knitting? I knit all the time. You should learn to knit. I bet if you did learn to knit, your stuff would look as stupid as you do."

Well, all righty, then.

And then there was the scorching mail from a nameless someone who wrote, "You should be fired for saying that knitting is for losers." (Just for the record, I did *not* say that. I implied it. Now crocheting and tatting? That's for losers. And don't even get me started on macramé. *Kidding!*)

Another writer took a more ominous approach: "You said knitters should 'get a life.' That wasn't very nice. You are a very crappy person, and maybe you shouldn't even have a life. Signed, Tony Soprano." (Okay, maybe not, but that's who it sounded like. Is there some kind of knitting Mafia out there? And, if so, do they stitch tiny little cozies for their Uzis? ("You have spoken disrespectfully of my hobby. And now you must pay. . . . Oh, criminy! How do I get this thing *off?*")

And this from another nutty knitter: "I suppose when you want to give a sweater to someone you love, you just go to the store and buy one!"

Well, uh, yes, Mrs. *Colonial House,* and your point would be?

The whole thing makes me wonder if I've tapped into some kind of Angry Knitters alternate universe. ("Don't mess with me. I *knit!*") I thought that knitting was supposed to relax you, rather like how watching an aquarium can lower your blood pressure. Although I'm not sure I believe that. I watch an aquarium and just get hungry for something yummy with slaw and hushpuppies.

Finally, I heard from a male knitter who said that he knits tiny little caps for premature babies, and he wanted to know what exactly I do for tiny little babies.

Well, admittedly, there's not much market for sarcasm among newborns, but, if it makes you feel better, I shall be happy to read aloud portions of my work to the unborn in wombs across America, rather like those Mozart tapes you're supposed to play to make your kid smart.

Just don't blame me if he comes out a smart-ass. You *so* asked for it, dude.

28

OnStar Hotline

Sure, They Can Help with Car Emergencies, but Can They Make a Decent Gravy?

"OnStar Hotline, may I help you?"

"Oh, thank God! *[panicky]* I need help with my Christmas list."

"Okay, ma'am, please calm down. I can see from your location that you are in the mall parking lot and your blood pressure has just spiked to a rather dangerous level."

"Well, that's because some doofus just took my parking space. *[sobbing]* You don't know what it's like out here, OnStar."

"Right, ma'am, we also see that it appears that your credit card has maxed out, so perhaps shopping isn't a good idea today. Ma'am."

"OnStar, I thought you were here to help."

"Right, ma'am, sorry to editorialize. Have your airbags deployed?"

"It's not a wreck, you ninny. It's a shopping emergency."

"Sorry again. Now, ma'am, it appears that, in fact, the pants you are wearing today do make your butt look too big."

"OnStar!"

"Sorry again, ma'am. We're really much better when it comes to auto emergencies, of which this doesn't seem to be one."

"Oh, right. Like the commercial where the woman has locked her keys in the car and her baby's inside and she's crying. That one always makes me cry when y'all unlock the doors."

"Me, too, ma'am."

"Really?"

"Of course not."

"OnStar, you're so good at helping everybody. Can you or can you not help me with my Christmas list?"

(Pause)

"OnStar, are you there?"

"Thinking, ma'am. Are you sure you don't have any kind of auto emergency? We're really quite well-trained to say things in comforting tones like, 'Sit tight! Help is on the way.'"

"And I love the commercial where you ask if the person in the wreck would like you to stay on the line until help arrives. That's just so sweet. I mean you're like a best friend in a box, on selected GM models, that is."

"Oh, now, keep going on, ma'am, and you're gonna have me bawling!"

"Right. What about help with my Christmas list—can you do it, OnStar?"

"Hmm. You know, fragrance is always nice. We at On-Star are partial to anything in the pine tree line or perhaps new car scent."

"I dunno, OnStar. Look, let's change subjects. Since you are so calm and comforting and knowledgeable, can you give me some advice so my turkey gravy isn't lumpy this year?"

"Whoa. You're asking the impossible now, ma'am. Everyone knows you make terrible gravy."

"They do? Everyone? How do you know?"

(Irritated sigh)

"Oh, right. You know everything."

"Now you're starting to get it, ma'am. Although, just between you and me, it wouldn't kill you to use cornstarch instead of flour. Oh, and, two words, Kitchen Bouquet. That shit is awesome!"

"OnStar! Did you just say *it-shay?*"

"Forgive me, ma'am. I got caught up in the moment. It won't happen again."

"Sure, fine. One more question, though. If you know so

much, can you tell me why people still pay money to hear
Ashlee Simpson sing when everyone knows she lip-synchs?"

(Silence)

"OnStar? Are you there?"

"Thinking, ma'am. Frankly, we at OnStar are surprised
at all the nepotism in the entertainment world. Another
caller wanted to know why Jamie Lynn Spears has her own
TV show. It's not as if there's a giant talent pool coming out
of Bigfoot, Louisiana, or wherever."

"Exactly, OnStar! I've been thinking the same thing
myself. Look, I know I've taken too much of your time already—"

"Well, ahem, that's okay, ma'am. Martha Stewart will
have to wait."

"*Martha Stewart?!* Is she on hold now?"

"Oh, dear. I didn't mean to name-drop like that. But,
yes, while you've been fretting over your gravy and your
Christmas list, a certain Connecticut homemaking mogul
has been waiting, it says here, rather impatiently for some
OnStar assistance."

"Oh, OnStar! Go help her! Martha needs you! I mean I
just love Martha and I think it was horrible that she went to
the big house, the pokey, stir, Oz, up the river—"

"Yes, we get it, ma'am."

"I'll admit, though, that I used to want to be just like
Martha, but then I read where she gets up before dawn, and
I was like, *screw* that! I mean you gotta love a woman who

gets up every Christmas morning at three a.m. just to wring the neck of her pet duck and stuff it with a mix of lightly braised shallots and human hearts. I mean, don't you?"

"Ma'am, I really have to go now. Ms. Stewart is starting to get upset. My GPS shows that she is going into a bit of a rage. Frankly, ma'am, I'm about to wet myself."

"Oh, of course. I understand. Just one more thing. This isn't going to turn into one of those OnStar commercials, is it, where y'all use the real-life emergency calls to sell your service?"

"Dream on, ma'am."

29

If It Ain't on eBay, It Ain't Worth Having

Whoa! Is That Willie Nelson's Face in Your Grits?

I read that Britney Spears's pregnancy test is for sale on eBay, perhaps inspired by the success of the sale of a wad of chewed gum she tossed during a London concert three years ago that went for fifty-three dollars.

One wonders why Britney can't just use a trash can like the rest of us, but apparently she just tosses and spits and flicks like crazy. Her cast-off Kleenexes and cigarette butts were also on eBay, in case you think the gum and pregnancy test are tacky. There's also a used bar of soap and a soiled hand towel deemed "priceless" by its owner, hmm, a Mr. J. Timberlake out of Memphis, Tennessee, perhaps?

People magazine reported that a cameraman at one of Britney's Canadian concerts snagged the wad of gum discarded backstage to show his friends and, after their interest waned (approximately three seconds later), he decided to try his luck on eBay.

Although there's no real way to prove that the gum has Britney's actual dried saliva and teeth impressions on it, short of calling in Marg Helgenberger and the rest of those *CSI* freaks, the seller offers "sorta proof" such as ticket stubs that show he attended a Britney concert sometime somewhere and perhaps a picture of Britney chewing actual gum.

Because Britney is such a prolific gum-chewer, it's a good idea to consider quitting your day job and just stalking her, waiting for the next wad of Juicy Fruit or Big Red to come flying across the hedgerow and into your waiting, gloved hands.

I, for one, won't be spending my hard-earned cash on Britney's alleged nose-blow. Not when I could be saving it up for something truly valuable like, say, spinach, flung from the tooth of The Rock (or "The," as I like to call him), my secret crush. Now *that's* money well spent.

Of course, you don't have to be famous to have something worth sharing with eBay. Diane Duyser of Florida made twenty-eight thousand dollars from the sale of a partially eaten ten-year-old grilled cheese sandwich that she said bore the image of the Virgin Mary.

The half-sandwich had spent the past decade nestled among a dozen cotton balls in a clear plastic case on Ms. Duyser's nightstand. Ms. Duyser, a devout woman with deeply held religious beliefs, said in a prepared statement that she wants all people to know that she believes that "This is the Virgin Mary, Mother of God." Still, apparently practicality won out. I mean, having the Mother of God on your nightstand along with your Jergens lotion and *TV Guide* is cool, but it doesn't really get that upstairs bathroom renovated, now does it?

Of course, it's not for me to judge Ms. Duyser's sincerity. I've seen the holy sandwich in pictures and, while there is definitely the blackened crumb outline of a woman's face in the bread, it really looks a whole lot more like Delta Burke to me.

But face it. Who's going to pay twenty-eight thousand dollars for a sandwich with Delta Burke's face on it? Believe me. Next time I splash cat food onto that Styrofoam plate and it looks even an itsy-tiny bit like the Virgin Mary, I'm alerting the media.

Thing is, these "miracles" tend to happen when you least expect them. Just last week, I sprinkled some Bugles on a paper towel for my daughter and her friend, and the way they fell out, they looked exactly like Johnny Depp.

Religious icons sell better, probably. Give me time. Today Johnny Depp, tomorrow Jerry Falwell, and then right on up to the Blessed Virgin. I once spotted Franklin Graham's face in a puddle of ranch dressing, but I was too hungry to do anything about it like the savvy Ms. Duyser.

One reason many people consider this a real miracle is

that the sandwich has never sprouted a single mold spore in ten years. This has got to be divine intervention. If I accidentally leave a lone Frito out overnight, it'll be covered with more hair than Robin Williams's forearms by morning.

The biggest mystery to me was how Ms. Duyser could eat just one bite of a grilled cheese sandwich and then have the willpower to put it aside. But then I found out it was made without any butter or oil. Hell-o. That's *not* a grilled cheese sandwich; that's blasphemy.

The winning eBay bidder turned out to be the owners of an on-line casino, who declared they'd spend "as much as it took" to own the holy toast.

Something tells me they've already gotten burned.

And, finally, let's consider the case of burly computer technician Larry Star of Seattle, who sold his ex-wife's wedding gown on eBay after writing a long and hilarious portrait of their married life together and posing for the photo wearing the gown.

Since the gown sold for $3,850 (about three times what he says it cost him five years ago), Larry might be on to something. He certainly surpassed his stated goal of making enough money for "beer and a couple of Mariners tickets."

Inspired by Larry's success, I went up into the old attic myself and found an autograph book with David Soul's autograph (the original Hutch, you know, and he drew a little peace sign inside the *o* in his last name—outtasite!), my black sequined prom dress, circa 1974, and what appears to be a possum skeleton. Let's start the bidding!

Larry, whose French-braidable back hair would probably send *Queer Eye* grooming guru Kyan Douglas reaching for his smelling salts, poked fun at his ex and her family and thanked the sweet Lord above that at least they hadn't had children. (Oopsie, well, yes, they did have a son as it turns out but it's a lot funnier the other way.)

After all the media attention—Larry was on talk shows more often than that psychic who wears the blue eye shadow—he's decided that he should write humor for a living.

To which I say, good luck, my furry friend. Larry could easily become the male counterpart to fictional but fabulous Carrie Bradshaw, relationships columnist on the old *Sex and the City*. A one-trick pony (chick-bashing), perhaps, but if it's funny, I'm in.

A word of warning to Larry, though. Be prepared for people to take you seriously. That line about how you will be wearing "a hairy, flesh-toned ensemble" for your next wedding because you'll be "buck naked with a toe tag lying on a slab in the morgue because I would have killed myself" will provoke a bunch of earnest letters from folks who bash you for making light of suicide.

It's all part of the job, Larry, and I won't lose any sleep fretting that you might get your feelings hurt. If you can laugh off the woman who told you she wished that she had her ex's testicles to sell on eBay, you're obviously not the sensitive sort.

At any rate, I appreciate you getting me thinking, Larry. Somewhere there's a couple out there with our names who would just love to have some more personalized wedding-bell cocktail napkins. Heck, I'll even throw in the possum skeleton. What am I bid?

30

Marketing Madness

It's Enough to Make You Lose Your (Poli)Grip

I don't recall when the big corporations started slowly, insidiously renaming the stadiums and arenas across this great nation, which, incidentally, is brought to you by Pepsi. But I do remember when it hit home. Just up the road from where I live, the pastoral concert venue Walnut Creek Pavilion was changed to the Alltel Pavilion thanks to a fat cash infusion from the cell phone giant. I still call it Walnut Creek. This is still a free (Dodge Ram) country after all.

The economic reality is that there are scores of renamed and rehabbed stadiums and concert halls all over the country. And aren't those shiny new skyboxes worth the humiliation of admitting that you actually bought tickets to the

Frito-Lay Bean Dip Rose Bowl or the Dr. Scholl's Corn Pads Fiesta Bowl?

It's hardly news that big money can change everything, but every now and then, say, while watching the WNBA's Light Days Panty Liner play of the game, I think that things have gone too far.

Oh, I was just kidding. Nobody watches the WNBA.

On the other hand, maybe if absolutely everything is for sale, why not me? Baby needs new shoes, as they say, and what I need is some corporate sponsorship. Why not the fruit-juicy Hawaiian Punch–line of the day? Are you listening PepsiCo?

For a little extra dough, I could insert into my books, talks, and humor columns veiled, subliminal messages that would be great free advertising for my corporate sponsors. My doctor says Mylanta. Okay, maybe more subtle than that.

Don't blame me. This is, like cross-country two-way communications by Nextel, the way of the future. Hons, you know it won't be long before Brian Williams thanks us for watching NBC's continuing coverage of the Sonic Jalapeño Poppers War in Iraq.

We're so conditioned to corporate sponsorship, who among us would be all that surprised to see the Swiffer WetJet "moppin' up the terrorists" moment of the day? The Toilet Duck "tank roll of the hour?" The Monistat "Yes, Geraldo was a fungus among us" field report?

The possibilities are as endless as the relief I always get

from Icy Hot. Purina could sponsor those moments when *American Idol* judge Randy Jackson affectionately calls someone "dawg."

As in Mighty Dog! Now with more tender kibbles and bits.

Although stadiums have sold out across the country, surprisingly, sanity prevailed when Major League Baseball decided (after allegations of monumental tackiness) not to place red-and-yellow *Spider-Man 2* promo ads on the bases at a Yankees game. At first MLB officials didn't seem to get it. They did, after all, pinkie-swear not to put anything on the hallowed home plate.

But they did plan to transform the on-deck circles into huge spiderwebs for the game.

It's small wonder that companies like Sony warmed to the idea. Sony is the parent of Columbia Pictures (and a rather permissive parent at that, the kind that never minded if you, heh-heh, had an underage beer when you visited your buddy on Hamburger Helper night). With so many people zapping commercials these days by using digital video recorders like TiVo, you have to be creative in promoting your product.

Maybe that explains the ham-handed product placement in *Cheaper by the Dozen,* a two-hour Crate & Barrel ad starring Steve Martin and Bonnie Hunt. Empty boxes with the nifty and unmistakable C & B logo were scattered in every room of the Baker house. Sure enough, when the brood moved uptown, the moving van was followed closely by the huge Crate & Barrel delivery truck. I think it backfired; now I associate owning C & B stuff with having twelve children. I'd rather eat my own eyeballs.

Subtle product placement is a thing of the past. If *Gone with the Wind* were made today, Clark Gable would pull Vivien Leigh close to say, "Frankly, Scarlett, I don't give a damn, but if I did, I'd choose Cingular Wireless with no roaming fees or activation costs."

For the first time in its hundred-year history, the Kentucky Derby is allowing jockeys to wear advertisements on their silks.

It's one thing to see Dale Jr. and his ilk coating themselves shamelessly in Viagra and Tide detergent decals but the Derby?

I don't blame the jockeys, who don't make all that much money, if you believe Spider-Man. Sorry, wrong Tobey Maguire movie. After all, they could be paid thirty thousand dollars to wear a little Wrangler jeans logo. Still, it tackies up everything and makes the world just a little bit more crass, a little less decent. Then again, what's my point? Did I mention that I'm for sale?

Major League Baseball officials changed their minds thanks to the pressure of fans, those oft-forgotten families who shell out ninety dollars for so-so seats and overboiled hot dogs.

Only a few days earlier, MLB had boasted that "*Spider-Man* is a natural fit for baseball," a wacky statement that made about as much sense as "Why, yes, Mr. Billy Joel, I'd be delighted to let you drive me home!"

It's been tough times for a lot of big business, so I guess they're getting desperate. Telemarketers can't hassle us anymore now that we've got the Do Not Call registry. I was one of the first of an estimated ten million angry Americans who signed up to have their phone number removed from telemarketers' call lists. Within months, some sixty million were signed up. The rest, I presume, are clinically insane.

The process is blissfully simple. With a few computer keystrokes, I could practically see the legions of telemarketers, with their offers of "free" water-quality testing, home security systems, groceries, and so forth fleeing like those zombies in the low-interest credit card commercial.

And that's not all. Now that I'm registered, I can sue any telemarketer who calls me for eleven thousand dollars per harassing call. This is going to be some fun, particularly if that perky pest from the time-share group in Williamsburg, Virginia, calls again. The last time she woke me on a Saturday morning to tell me that Williamsburg was waiting for me to see firsthand the "magical marriage of perfectly preserved history and modern-day fun," I told her that if I ever meet her in person, she better make sure there aren't any loaded muskets lying around.

Sadly, the don't-call list doesn't filter out all household pests, just 80 percent of them. Charities are exempt, even the phony ones.

This means the Quasi Fraternal Benevolent Lovers of Law Enforcement, who harass me more than anyone else, can legally call me. These people are the most persistent, interrupting my dinner preparations nightly with "Hello, we'd like to keep drug dealers off the street, and we need your help."

This has led to the unbecoming sight of me standing at the stove as my young daughter quietly colors at the kitchen table while I scream into the phone "Leave me alone! I love drugs!" Nothing else has worked, so I have high hopes for this approach.

While there is some concern that the new don't-call laws will put many thousands of telemarketers out of a job, causing a serious jump in the nation's unemployed, I think I speak for many millions of Americans when I say, "So?"

31

My Last Meal?

That's Easy: A Clam Roll and a Dozen
Krispy Kremes (Oh, Hell, Keep 'Em Coming)

My friend Lisa, whom I always call Liser because she's from South Carolina (aka South Cackalackie), has a theory about the so-sad plunging of Krispy Kreme's fortunes.

Liser and I have spent an inordinate amount of time lately fretting about the fate of Krispy Kreme on account of *we can't live without them.*

If Keith Richards had gotten hooked on KKs instead of that pesky and harder-to-find heroin, he could've gone through life with actual cheeks.

Liser says that KK forgot its base, its core, its down-South faithful, and I think she's on to something. At first, we Southerners were excited and proud when we read about those über-bored, sophisticated Manhattanites dizzily lining up for "two glazed," flicking the inevitable shower of sugar from their black uniforms en route to their glamorous jobs. Maybe this would be the one thing that could unite Southerners and Northerners. After all, grits haven't worked out like we'd hoped. I still blush at the memory of ordering grits in Atlantic City, New Jersey, and having the waitress look at me, laugh heartily, and finally say, "Grit? What is grit?"

"It's not singular," I'd said with as much Southern pride as I could assemble on short notice. "It's grits."

She laughed even harder.

Although the Yankees who move down South find plenty of fault with much of what we do and how we act, they have never failed to understand, once they taste one, that Krispy Kreme doughnuts are the finest things on God's green earth.

No sane person would dis KKs once they've tried a hot one. A recent transplant once told me that Dunkin' Donuts tasted better, but I knew there was only one plausible explanation for that kind of foolish talk.

"You haven't actually tried a hot Krispy Kreme, have you?" I asked.

"Well, no, but Dunkin' Donuts has always been the best."

"Try one, and get back to me," I said with more kindness than I felt. Truthfully, I was nearly as angry as I was the time a Yankee woman who was visiting a Southern friend of mine announced that our pork barbecue "tastes just like vomit."

I wanted to kill her with my bare hands but it wouldn't have been Christian.

A few days later, there was an e-mail from Mr. Dunkin' Donuts: "I'm so sorry about what I said. We tried them and have been back every night since."

Well, of course.

So when we in the South kept hearing about the phenomenal success of Krispy Kreme up north and beyond, we wondered: Could this be the bridge between cultures that we've been missing ever since the Waw-wuh? Would our Northern neighbors pay proper homage at first bite as all good Southerners do by saying, "Mmmm-mmm. Now *that's* what I'm talkin' about!"

But something went wrong, and Krispy Kreme, the business, is in a severe downward spiral for inflating sales figures and other Martha Stewarty crimes. Thinking they were Starbucks (the coffee's okay, but you'll chip a tooth on that biscotti), they overbuilt stores like crazy, borrowed too much, and used some accounting techniques that would make Donald Trump blush to keep stockholders happy.

Although nobody's come out and said it, you could summarize KK's problems with a simple and oft-used Southernism: They got above their raisin'.

All that success made them forget their simple roots: wonderfully tacky green-and-white stores in small Southern cities where local high school students could buy cartons at the back door to raise money for the yearbook, band uniforms, lights for the stadium, whatever.

I remember loading my old Chevy II with dozens of boxes and driving them forty miles home, where they sold in about twelve seconds at the gas station.

But then Sarah Jessica Parker got caught eating one and acting like she *discovered* them. My Aunt Fannie.

As movie stars raved, KK stores sprang up like dollarweed across the whole country, and we Southerners watched with a mix of pride and trepidation.

Liser says, wisely, that Krispy Kremes are special because every Southerner has a memory of them. Mine mostly involve highly illegal traffic maneuvers such as jumping a median and making a U-turn after seeing that sacred moment when the HOT DOUGHNUTS NOW! sign flickers on.

Did Moses ignore the burning bush? Did the wise men say, "Nice star, but we've really got some laundry to do?" I think not.

Sadly, with mass production came a drop in standards. Doughnuts sold up Nawth came with instructions for reheating. Say who? Any right-thinking Southerner knows that Krispy Kremes must be eaten hot, preferably at the cash register while you're still fishing for change.

It's not that they're bad cold; it's just that they're ordinary, which is something they should never, ever be.

Liser's theory that we love Krispy Kreme because of the

memories must be the reason that I'm so devastated at the closing of a decidedly un-Southern restaurant chain.

Howard Johnson represented the very best of my childhood: road-trip vacations that always included a stop at HoJo for "frankfurters grilled in butter," fried clam strips in a butter-soaked roll shaped like a boat, and a kids' menu that was perforated so that, after ordering, you could punch out the lines and wear it as a hat.

Howard Johnson, with its iconic orange room, turquoise trim, and Simon the Pieman logo, was the first place I ever ate coconut ice cream, and it was love at first bumpety bite. I've had it plenty of times since, but it has never tasted so good.

Howard Johnson in Boston was the first place my young Southern eyes saw a tableful of nurses, still in their uniforms and just off work, happily swilling beer and cussing up a storm.

Whoa. The only nurse I knew was the one who took my temperature and patted my hand at the doctor's office in my tiny hometown.

Because this was the South, the doctor's office had a few unfortunate furnishings. Aside from the distressing "colored" and "white" waiting rooms that remained all the way into the 1970s, there was a terrifying display of jars containing malformed cow fetuses and the like.

That nurse from my childhood had steel-gray hair and

never cussed or drank anything stronger than a Dr Pepper, although I can tell you if I had to stare at those cow fetuses all day, I'd probably be on the pipe in less than a week.

So I watched these strong workingwomen with booming laughter like they were some new life-form, which, to a Southern tadpole, they were.

I was so busy eavesdropping, I could barely concentrate on another staple in the long HoJo list of weird favorites: Boston baked beans and brown bread, sitting in a steaming trademark brown crock in front of me.

On the way out, you could always buy the brown bread in a can with the HoJo logo on it. Bread in a can? Cussing nurses? Let's just say my world was rocked.

Howard Johnson's in Winston-Salem, North Carolina, was the place where I saw Roger McGuinn and some of The Byrds enjoying what I now realize was preconcert "high food."

I marveled at the good fortune of seeing somebody famous and double-marveled at how they could eat that many French fries. Yes, well. I was very young.

At Howard Johnson's in Jacksonville, North Carolina, I celebrated an engagement that (mercifully) never got off the ground. You could question the wisdom of choosing Howard Johnson's for such a lofty occasion, but this was the '70s, and things were different then. We didn't have pesto.

So, yes, I'm devastated that HoJo has closed all but eight of its original 850 restaurants. The experts say it's no surprise, because of the chain's old buildings, a menu that never changed, and too much competition from those noisy box restaurants that brag about serving margaritas in a fish bowl. To hell with them. They can't make a decent clam roll.

With all the diet hysteria, I guess we shouldn't be surprised that these old-school chains like Krispy Kreme and HoJo are suffering. Maybe it's just as well that they go out gracefully. I'd have hated to see HoJo have to change its famous Indian pudding to Native American pudding or transform its beloved $1.49 fish fry night into a sushi special.

Can I get an Amen?

32

Politicians Serve Up McValues

(With Extra Cheese on the Side)

Why is it that every election year, politicians on both sides insist on trying to convince me that they share my "values." Usually, they don't get specific but rather toss out big, dumb puffy-cloud piffle that doesn't mean much of anything.

Yeah, yeah, I get that every time you trot out the V-word I'm supposed to get a rumbling in my chest that has nothing to do with that unfortunate burrito decision made earlier in the day and everything to do with old-fashioned purple mountains' majesty patriotism.

Of course they must share my values because there they are in the campaign ads, shirt-sleeves rolled up neater than *Queer Eye*'s Carson, happily hugging perky soccer moms and gooey-perfect round babies. (And speaking of soccer moms, how do they all know how to do that knotted sweater thing

where the sweater just casually flows from their shoulders?
I tried that and damn near hanged myself.)

With all the crowing about values, it won't be long before the candidate coos "I share your values, yes, um do"
into the ear of yet another overweight American toddler.
Memo to politician: This kid eats Legos and sand all day. Is
this really someone you want to cozy up to?

So what are our Values? What do we truly hold dear in a
nation where you can actually order off the McValue menu?
Once we've gotten past the Big Three—faith, family, and
Fear Factor—we get to the nittus-grittus, and that, my hons,
is where I come in.

I made a little list of things of things I value that I'd like
to see the politicians embrace.

Banana pudding as the National Dessert. I don't know if
we have a national dessert, but if we do, it's probably something stupid and moldy that Dolley Madison whipped up
back when everything was made with raisins and wood.

Sweet iced tea, even at Starbucks. Take that infernal,
overpriced mango-infused goo you're pretending to like so
much and flush it down your ergonomic potty. (P.S. What
the hell is a *barista*? This is America, you idiots, call them
what they are: counter help.)

Children who scream in public places for no good reason.
If your kids can't behave in public, for heaven's sake do what
your grandmother did, and give 'em some Benadryl. Hey,
it's not rocket science. A sleepy kid is far less likely to have

the energy to chase his sister around the Target rounders with a newly mined booger, as I witnessed recently.

Immediate firing of any restaurant employee who says "No problem" when I ask for something. No problem? Well, one would hope not since *it's your job and all*.

People who don't get the joke. Any joke. I hate to tell you how much heat I took for suggesting that Hong Kong scientists could make more progress on SARS if they'd use actual PETA members for their experiments.

Those inane privacy notices that come with every piece of mail these days. The other day I received one with a bill from a doctor's office. It said: "We do not sell your private information to anyone!" Rather than using a tone that implies that medals and pie should be awarded for this, shouldn't we be able to assume that? I would hope that they also don't kick old people and small dogs in the face "just because."

But, most of all, I want to live long enough to see elections where candidates give me more than a bunch of patriotic platitudes. Is that really too much to ask?

Maybe yes. I met William J. Bennett seven years ago at a naturalization ceremony for several dozen brand-new American citizens. Even for a jaded newsie, it was hard not to choke up while watching them file by a huge, flag-draped trash can and ceremoniously toss in little flags representing their native countries.

In the speech that followed, Bennett extolled the virtues of the Good American: honesty, hard work, self-discipline, and the ability to successfully double down without looking like a monkey at the blackjack tables.

Bennett, a former "drug czar," which, in actual fact, does *not* require him to wear a funny pointy hat, is the self-appointed King of Virtues. So imagine my surprise to learn that he'd lost $8 million playing video poker. *Video poker.* Not even a classy James Bondian game like baccarat, which requires shirt and shoes. Video poker? It reminds me of those old men I used to see in Atlantic City who'd spend all day betting quarters on motorized plastic horses racing around an Astroturf-covered table.

I don't know. For a former U.S. Secretary of Education, it's just so, well, un-czarlike.

You could argue that Bennett spent his own money pursuing a leisure activity in legally operated casinos. He even pointed out that he didn't put his family "at risk" or "spend the milk money."

Hell, I know the guy's insanely rich. He probably didn't even spend the "ski retreat in Vail" money. The rich, hons, are not like you and me. They have never known the sweaty anticipation of scratching off the numbers on the tic-tac-dough lotto tickets after driving ninety minutes to the Citgo station just across the state line in South Carolina. I mean, not me, of course, but friends of mine.

So what if Bennett lost more than $500,000 in Vegas one day? It was his to lose, right?

I don't know. Maybe I'm just bitter. After all, nowhere in my daughter's copy of Bennett's bestselling *Children's Book of Virtues* does it mention anything really useful. Instead of the blather about how "a brave heart will always persevere as long as it takes to get the job done," why not tell us something we can truly use, like how to persevere to get the best five-card hand so we can earn the bonus with our payout?

Instead of the heartwarming tale of the little Dutch boy saving his town by holding his finger in the dike, why not tell us how to sniff out the best slots at Harrah's?

Education schmeducation. As long as you work on your Joker Poker playing skills, you might as well use that high school diploma to wipe the wing grease off your chin at drink-free-till-you-pee night at the casino.

Virtue is its own reward, as they say. But you don't get your room comped with virtue, right, Billy boy?

If I sound jaded about politicians, is it any wonder? I mean, they're just so abominably ordinary. Except maybe for Strom Thurmond, who finally died, but I hear they had him stuffed and he's working as a greeter at the North Myrtle Beach Wal-Mart. What with fathering out-of-wedlock children with his African American mistress while spouting segregationist politics, you could never call him dull.

Ditto Dick Cheney, who knew his microphone was working and still invited a political rival to perform an unnatural anatomical act on himself. Cheney didn't apologize but did say he felt better for having said it.

I feel ya, Mr. Vice President. Who among us hasn't let fly with a few well-chosens in times of deep stress. When I do this, I'm a good enough Methodist to feel automatically ashamed of myself. Apparently, Cheney is just a manly man blowing off some steam.

While Cheney sparked a furor with his "ugly talk," Teresa Heinz Kerry got pounded by the mommies after she appeared to fairly jerk poor little Jack Edwards's thumb from his mouth during a campaign stop. I joined other mommies across the nation in a bobble-headed chorus of "Oh, no, she *did-unt.*"

Teresa crossed the Mommy Line when she swatted at the four-year-old's hand while his own mom stood just inches away. It's not like she's his memaw, which, as we all know, is the only universally recognized "stand in" administrator of parental discipline.

Mommies get squirrely when somebody tries to discipline their kids, even if that somebody is right. Most of us resist the urge, though powerful at times, to point out that Little Johnny was surely raised by wolves.

As a Southern mommy, Elizabeth Edwards should have felt free to say, "Back off, ketchup queen, this doesn't concern you." Perhaps Teresa would have invited her to "shove it," and then the real fun would begin!

The truth is, it's strangely refreshing to hear people in

power say what they really think, no matter how crude. It has provided some comic relief from the pious values and virtues pabulum. What's that? You think civil political discourse that adheres to the rules of living in polite society is all that separates us from the savages? Oh, just go Cheney yourself, I say.

Cussing politicians. Meddling mamas. Gambling-addicted moral authorities. Just when you think politics can't get any weirder, you find yourself saying three words that you thought you never would: Governor Arnold Schwarzenegger.

Although he's no longer the darling of his constituents, Ahnold is said to be eyeing the Oval Office if he can just get around that bothersome Constitutional thingy that prevents "furriners" from being president.

I'm envisioning a cabinet that might include Secretary of State Jean-Claude Van Damme or perhaps Attorney General Jackie Chan.

When Arnold was elected governor of his beloved "Cally-fawn-ee-ya," I thought they had to be kidding. He had so many sexual harassment lawsuits filed against him, it was just too Kobe-licious to consider.

I couldn't believe that Californians elected a guy whose résumé listed his greatest political achievement as "marrying famous Kennedy chick." It didn't even hurt him when somebody dug up an old interview in which he essentially said Adolf Hitler was as cute as a basket of kittens.

California's historic switching of gubernatorial horses in

midstream has led other states to wonder if they should follow suit, asking, "Hey, why can't we have a muscle-bound, knuckleheaded movie star to lead us into the future and shit?"

I live in a state with a decent enough governor. He's earnest and hardworking, but let's face it, he's no George Clooney. I like the man, personally, but, truth be told, what we really need in North Carolina is native son Andy Griffith, who was wise as both Sheriff Andy Taylor *and* Ben Matlock. If he's too frail, we've still got Michael Jordan, who would make damn sure we'd finally get our lottery. (Are you listening, Bennett?)

As crazy as it sounds, Californians clearly confused Arnold's tough Terminator-speak with the real person. Who better to open up a can of whup-ass on high taxes and a limp economy than an action hero? The worm turned, as it often does in politics, and Arnold's approval ratings dived when everyone found out that he wasn't close to superhuman and he'd never be able to save the world.

At least not unless he could get those Charlie's Angels to help him.

Epilogue

Oh, don't y'all just love this part of a book? Sometimes I read it first because I want to make sure everything turns out okay. Whether it's a novel or nonfiction, the epilogue is that fabulous little business at the end that tells you, with great authority and certainty "whatever happened to . . ."

Loose ends are tied up, questions are answered, and you can close the book with a satisfying *thwump* and get on with your life feeling as merrily stuffed as if you'd just eaten a dish of warm peach cobbler. Well, almost.

If my life were a novel—and, really, what Southern life isn't?—I'd want the final epilogue to say something like, "She moved to a big old house on the beautiful Battery in Charleston, where she lives with her adoring husband, devoted daughter, plumber son-in-law (it's an old house in the South, remember?), and three excruciatingly attractive and well-mannered grandchildren. She eats Lowcountry Shrimp and Grits at least four days a week and twice't on Sundays and, as far as regrets, only wishes she could take back that time when she yelled at her six-year-old so loudly that a huge pecan tree limb shattered and landed between them.

The incident, which might have been interpreted by some as a sign from the Almighty to lighten up a bit, merely made her consider a new career path. She considered hiring herself out, making extra money by going to people's houses and screaming at their unwanted limbs: "Pick up your toys!" "Don't yank on my clothes while I'm talking on the phone!" "Finish your math homework!" "Stop eating all my Cheez Waffies!"

Southern women are notoriously resourceful, and screaming at foliage is a whole lot better than yelling at your kids. Even if they did eat all your Cheez Waffies.

When you write about your life, you have to be willing to own up to the stuff that isn't so flattering, especially if it's funny.

When all my friends made noble-sounding New Year's resolutions this year, I simply pledged to upgrade my TiVo by year's end. I should have, instead, resolved to have a stronger work ethic. Okay, any work ethic would do.

Why can't I be more like Stephen King, famous for finishing thirty pages every day before a breakfast of, I'm guessing, a monkey-brain-and-bat's-blood omelet?

Or more like Dave Barry, whose clever use of words like *muskrat, boogers,* and *underpants* earned him a Pulitzer? For years, people have asked me why my newspaper columns aren't syndicated like Barry's, and I always tell the truth: Dave Barry is a once-in-a-lifetime talent who has honed his craft over many, many decades and who is also rumored to have an outstanding collection of photographs of newspaper syndicate executives committing unspeakable acts with farm animals.

What? What'd I say?

That's me, though, a frequent traveler on life's low roads. When I gave my sweet husband a T-shirt for Christmas that said I LIKE MY WOMEN LIKE MY COFFEE, GROUND UP AND IN THE FREEZER, he looked, well, frightened.

If I'm ever going to get that house on the Battery, y'all are going to have to step up and buy a bunch of these books. Hey, I'm not asking for me; think of the grandchildren.

It's not like success would ruin me, hons. I would still be the same bitchy chick with a heart as big as a slop jar that y'all have been kind enough to put up with through three—count 'em, three—collections of Southern strangeness.

I'm not going to be one of those eccentric Southerners who lets a little success go to her head. Never! And rumors that I once showed up for a book signing and demanded a dressing room stocked with 12 cases of Diet Mountain Dew, 60 cans of squeeze cheese, and 118 boxes of Waverly Wafers are just hateful lies!

With fame should come an entourage, and I positively can't wait for mine! True story: One time I saw Martin Lawrence in person. He was making a movie on my street and he had a *huge* entourage, including a muscular man whose only duty was to answer Martin's cell and gently hold it to his ear and two women who allowed him to rest his noggin on their huge chests in between takes like they were a collection of Koosh pillows.

Okay, never mind the entourage. I don't need a bunch of hangers-on tending to my every need. Just one will do, as long as his name is Mr. Matthew McConaughey.

That's it. You can *thwump* now. Peace out.

Acknowledgments

This book wouldn't exist without two people who continue to have faith in the funny: Jenny Bent, my incomparable agent, and Jennifer Enderlin, my brilliant editor. Their wisdom and support sustain and nurture me, and I thank them from the bottom of my heart.

I'm indebted to the entire team at St. Martin's Press, including John Karle, my adorable publicist and an excellent listener; talented designer Sarah Delson; Kim Cardascia, who answers all my silly questions; media escorts Pat Speltz (who introduced me to Memphis ribs, the best food on God's earth), "Kentucky" Barb Ellis (who sniffed out the Talbots outlet for me and I've got the eight-dollar sandals to prove it!), Michelle Dunn, and Lenore Markowitz; and the hardworking, dedicated sales and distribution staff. Bless you all.

Acknowledgments

Special thanks to Mark Kohut, who introduced me to the spectacular folks at Ingram in Nashville, Tennessee. I've never had a better audience!

Over the years, so many booksellers have offered encouragement, advice, and, best of all, a nice, tall stack of books right beside the cash register. I'm especially grateful for the enthusiastic support of Nicki Leone of Bristol Books in Wilmington, North Carolina, who has helped me in more ways than I can list and who reminds me that anything's funny as long as you can insert the word *monkey* somewhere. She's right, of course. Because of Nicki, I am tinkering with the idea for my first novel, *The Da Vinci Monkey*.

I'm deeply grateful for the support of booksellers Cathy Stanley of Two Sisters Bookery as well as Deborah Goodman and the staff of Barnes & Noble in Wilmington, North Carolina, whose awesome wall-of-books display was so amazing, it made me cry.

Other booksellers who have gone above and beyond to promote my work include Nancy Olson and Renee Martin at Quail Ridge Books & Music in Raleigh; Lynn Payne, B & N, Charlotte; Larry Tyler, B & N, Myrtle Beach; Deon Grainger, Waldenbooks, Myrtle Beach; Kathy Patrick, Beauty & the Book, Jefferson, Texas; Katherine Whitfield, Davis-Kidd, Memphis; and Jamie Kornegay and all the fabulous folks at Square Books and Thacker Mountain Radio in beautiful Oxford, Mississippi.

Acknowledgments

Special thanks also to Wanda Jewell, executive director of the Southeast Booksellers Association, and the many members of SEBA who hand-sold my books to sunburned tourists from Virginia to Florida saying, "This is what we're about in the South."

I am deeply indebted to my newspaper, TV, and radio friends especially Colin Burch and the late Mike Morgan at the *Myrtle Beach Sun-News;* Amber Nimocks, Jeff Hidek, Amanda Kingsbury, Ben Steelman, and Allen Parsons at the *Wilmington Morning Star;* Robie Scott at the *Charleston* (SC) *Post & Courier;* Carolyn Gibson of WYPL FM, Memphis; and Betty Ann Sanders and Diane Stokes, TV hostesses extraordinaire.

Hugs and MoonPies to generous and talented authors Lee Smith, Jill McCorkle, Laurie Notaro, Haven Kimmel, and Haywood Smith, who have been kind enough to support me in front of God and everybody.

Keeping me nourished, body and soul, are my wonderful friends Lawton and Mabel Halterman, who share the bounty of their garden, including the best new potatoes and butterbeans on earth, and Lawrence Shadrach and his daughter, Bess, who keep me in gardenia bouquets every June. Their daylily garden next door is a vision I savor all summer long.

Thanks also to the delightful Ronda Rich for so graciously sharing her knowledge of the speakers' circuit with a rookie who still feels like throwing up right before.

Acknowledgments

For making me laugh, or making me think, this year, I give thanks to an assortment of friends, new and old, including Tim Russell, Courtney Grannan, Kara Chiles, Debbi Pratt, Susan Reinhardt, P. D. Midgett, Laura Mitchell, Vance Williams, and Bill Atkinson.

And, finally, especially and most of all, I'm grateful to my wonderful husband, Scott Whisnant, who would be perfect even if he didn't think that Angelina Jolie with her big ol' futon lips is overrated, and to our precious daughter, Sophie, who is smarter, funnier, and kinder than I and who is patiently teaching me how to swim and raise crickets. I love you big.

Don't Miss Celia's Other Books!

"**HILARIOUS**—and right on the money."
—*The Charlotte Observer*

"Even die-hard Yankees will appreciate this **WICKEDLY FUNNY** collection...an amusing and **REFRESHINGLY HONEST** look at family life...."
—*Dallas Morning News*

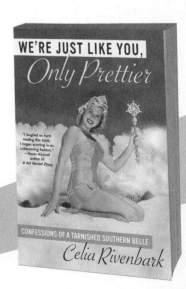

Available wherever books are sold.
www.celiarivenbark.com

 St. Martin's Griffin